KEY

1 Irish Tourist Office   (E.4)
2 General Post Office   (E.4)
3 Municipal Art Gallery   (D.5)
4 Catholic Pro-Cathedral   (E.4)
5 Civic Museum   (E.3)
6 O'Connell Bridge   (E.3, 4)
7 Custom House and Aras Mhic
   Dhiarmada (Bus Station) (F.4)
8 Bank of Ireland   (E.3)
9 Trinity College   (E, F.3)

10 Four Courts   (D.3, 4)
11 St Michan's Church   (C.3, 4)
12 Dublin Castle.   (D.3)
13 City Hall.   (D.3)
14 Christ Church Cathedral.   (D.3)
15 St Patrick's Cathedral.   (D.2)
16 { A. National Library,
      B. National Art Gallery.
      C. Leinster House.
      D. National Museum.
          (E, F.2, 3)

17 Government   ngs.   (E.2)
18 University Co   Dublin.
19 R.D.S. Show   ds. (G.1)
20 Kingsbridge S   (B.3)
21 Westland Rov   on. (F.3)
22 Amiens Street   on. (F.4)
23 Mansion House   3)

Based on the Ordnance Survey by permission of ernment (Perr

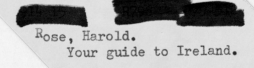

YOUR GUIDE TO IRELAND

Your Guide to
IRELAND

by

HAROLD ROSE

FUNK & WAGNALLS
NEW YORK

Library of Congress Catalog
Card Number: 68–18175

Published by Funk & Wagnalls
A Division of Reader's Digest Books, Inc.
by arrangement with Alvin Redman Limited

Printed in Great Britain by
D. R. Hillman & Sons Ltd.
Frome, Somerset

FOR BUNNY

CONTENTS

Part Four: NORTHERN IRELAND

ACKNOWLEDGEMENTS

I am most grateful for the kind assistance I received while writing this book: from Bord Fáilte Éireann (The Irish Tourist Board) in Dublin, and especially Mr. Terence J. Sheehy, B.F.E. General Manager in Britain, and his London office staff; from Mr. Robert Frizzell, General Manager of the Northern Ireland Tourist Board in Belfast, and Miss Patricia O'Neill, his representative at the Ulster Office in London; from Aer Lingus—Irish International Airlines, and particularly its Publicity Officer, Mr. R. F. Bate; from the various heroes of the hotel revolution I have mentioned in the book; and from the countless people I stopped all over the lovely country and who gave me the Irish smile, the warm welcome and the solution to my problems. Thanks to themselves, and to those invisible guardians of the peace that is Ireland, the Little People, all of whom also had a hand in the writing.

May, 1964   H.R.

11

ILLUSTRATIONS

Plate 1 is reproduced by courtesy of Aer Lingus. Plates 2 and 4–21 are reproduced by courtesy of the Irish Tourist Board; and plates 22–30 by courtesy of the Northern Ireland Tourist Board.

14

FOREWORD

Harold Rose, an experienced traveller in many lands, in this concise tourist guide to Ireland, pays tribute to what he terms the "relaxed efficiency" of tourism in Ireland and to the "various heroes of the hotel revolution".

In this volume the armchair traveller, and the potential tourist, will find details of the many varieties of holidays available in Ireland. Such major attractions as fishing, boating on uncrowded inland waterways, motoring on traffic-free roads, golfing on championship courses are among the many aspects of holidays in Ireland covered in this comprehensive guide.

It is evident that Mr. Rose has been completely captivated by the charm of Ireland. In conclusion he writes: "Ireland offers peace to everyone, but is particularly an angler's paradise. The combination of lake, line and rod, and all that wonderful quiet are likely to win me over very frequently . . ."

I sincerely hope that every reader who takes this handy, helpful guide to Ireland with him on his holidays to our country enjoys himself as much as Harold Rose does on his visits to this land of "One Hundred Thousand Welcomes".

Dr. T. J. O'Driscoll,
Director-General,
Bord Fáilte, the Irish Tourist Board,
Dublin.
May, 1964.

INTRODUCTION

Some of the Irish say you can see most of their country in a couple of weeks. And although it's themselves telling you, there never was a bigger load of blarney. Two weeks may be all right for a first visit, but you will need the same again each time you return. That is, if you ever leave. It is not easy to get away from this wonderful place. Everything is for you and against you, as it were! The glorious scenery, the unspoilt territory, the peaceful pace of life, and the kindly charming Irish—backed up as they are by the invisible hordes of Little People.

What chance has anyone in the face of such an assault on the senses? None. So then, you will want to go back again and again and I have no doubt that, knowing this to be a certainty, the Irish say you can cover the country in two weeks. It's all very subtle. And it makes a pleasant change, in one of the few countries where commercial overselling is unknown. It may even make some people sorry that their mothers did not come from Ireland.

Devoted as I am to Italy, it came as a shock to discover that I had to divide my loyalties between that country and Ireland. My immediate liking for a country so different from Italy is wrapped up in the character of its people. As J. M. Scott said in the *Sunday Telegraph:* "They are as interested in you as the Italians are."

Both nations are gay. The Italians rush to greet you with illustrious gestures, and the Irish eyes that really do smile diffuse that charm which softens without lessening a similar degree of enthusiasm. Latin Giorgio is often overpoweringly kind. Gaelic Patrick is a broth of a boy with a tiny restraint.

17

But this, due to a rather mischievous zest for life, quickly goes, as if it has been held in a bubble which bursts at the mere sight of you. So the differences are slight. The sincerity of the Irish is obvious—even those who doubt it are converted when they find that the many extra services resulting from a natural desire to please do not appear on the bill. The Irish give so much because they want to, and they are blessedly unique in doing so without any sense of servility.

Perhaps nowhere else has the peaceful nature of a country encouraged, instead of laziness, the steady progress of its people. If it was ever true that things happened slowly or not at all in Ireland, that time has passed. Cheerfulness no longer hides shortcomings. Amenities, particularly the brilliantly transformed hotels, are all run with relaxed efficiency. Like the Italians, the Irish are very good hoteliers. For this and countless other reasons, I have finally narrowed down my choice of holiday countries and the I's have it. One writer says there is a spiritual link: "A surprising number of Irish people have been to Rome." (He also thinks Ireland was part of Atlantis.)

There is probably no place where, officially, you can dig up antiquities and keep them for yourself. Ireland is no exception, but there, if you come across a leprechaun, you need not report it to the authorities. In a country full of tales, this is accepted—both as legend and fact, if you take my meaning. I am sure that one of the things which makes the Irish such charmers is that they believe in fairies. I go even further and suggest that the Irish people, having crashed the doubt barrier, are really leprechauns in disguise.

Wherever you meet them, they are delighted to see you. Patrick O'Donovan, in one of his *Observer* articles, said: "There is the hugged-in pleasure of a bar, where the men

talk quietly and well with a courtesy that we have forgotten."
He went on describing "an authentic nation with a strong
personal flavour of her own and one that has an over-
whelming sense of the imminence of hell and damnation
and yet manages marvellously to enjoy this vale of tears".

What makes them even more worthy is that they readily
share their beautiful part of the vale with you. To them,
you are as welcome as spring, at any time of the year.
Nothing will be too much trouble. It was good of you to
come.

At the end of my last visit, just before I finished writing
this book, the hotel manager said: "Thank you for staying
with us." In a world society that has become selfish, sour
and stupid, how nice it is to meet the Irish, the people God
has clearly chosen to show us the road back.

PART ONE

GENERAL INFORMATION

THIS IS IRELAND

If the surface of the sea were lowered only 300 feet, Ireland, and Britain, would become part of mainland Europe. Fortunately, both are islands—fortunately because this is a major reason why Ireland has escaped the smoke and the noise of industrialisation. The Irish often regret the fact, but it is their greatest advantage. It has left them untarnished by the rat-race, and given British and other tourists one of the most beautiful places they can visit anywhere in the world.

The total area of Ireland is 32,524 square miles, the greatest length is 302 miles, and the greatest width is 189 miles. No part of the country is more than 70 miles from the sea. The Republic of Eire consists of twenty-six counties covering 27,073 square miles, and divided into the provinces of Munster, Leinster and Connacht, as well as three counties of Ulster. At the 1956 census, its population was 2,898,264. The remaining six counties of Ulster are known as Northern Ireland, and have an area of 5,451 square miles, with a population, at the 1961 census, of 1,425,462. Eire is a democratic, independent state. Dublin, population 584,483, is the capital. Northern Ireland, controlled by a Parliament in Belfast, is subordinate to the British Parliament.

It is generally accepted that all the islands around Europe were once part of its land mass. Ireland is among them. The country has an undulating central plain ringed around almost completely by a coastal belt of highlands. In the central area, there are extensive bogs and glacial deposits of sand and clay. Numerous lakes are found here, too. (The country has 800 lakes and many rivers.) The central area is drained by the River Shannon, with a basin extending over one-fifth of the country. Red sandstone rocks are the main feature of the south and south-west regions, limestone covers the valleys and carries the main rivers which, in some places, cut across ridges through picturesque gorges. The ridges become mountains towards the west, and reach their maximum height in the county of Kerry.

The mountains have their effect on the climate, and the position of the island, facing the warm Atlantic, causes high rainfall, cool summers, mild winters and considerable wind. The wet climate has resulted in extensive development of the peat-bog on the plains, covering a seventh of the country, and providing the people with virtually endless supplies of fuel.

Most of the best scenery is in the coastal areas, especially in Connemara, Cork, Kerry, Mayo, Donegal and Wicklow. Ruggedly attractive too, are such topographical features as the limestone desert of the Burren in the northern part of County Clare; and the very dramatic Giant's Causeway in north-eastern Ireland.

Studies of the flora and fauna, and of the archaeology of the country, reveal many links with Britain and substantiate the belief that the two countries were once joined. It is to their separation, to the effects of the Ice Age, and of the rainfall, that Ireland owes much of her beauty.

PASSPORTS AND VISAS

British subjects need *no travel documents* for travel to Ireland. Visitors from Britain, the Commonwealth, the United States or West European countries require a valid passport but no visa.

CURRENCY

Any amount of sterling, dollars or other currency can be taken into Ireland, in cash, travellers' cheques or other forms of payment. Not more than £50 in British and/or Irish banknotes may be exported on leaving Ireland—except direct to Great Britain, the Channel Islands or the Isle of Man, in which cases there is no limit. Foreign currency notes can be exported up to the value of £250 ($700) in excess of the amount brought into Ireland.

British currency is in the same denominations as Irish money, and can be freely circulated in Ireland. Dollars are also accepted in most places, at the full rate of exchange. The rate between Irish, United States and Canadian currency varies slightly from time to time but is on the average $2.40 to £1.

Banks are open on Mondays to Fridays from 10 a.m. to 12.30 p.m. and 1.30 to 3 p.m. On Saturdays (except in towns where they close for a different half-day) they are open from 9.30 to 11.30 a.m. The principal banks are Bank of Ireland; Belfast Banking Co.; Hibernian; Munster and Leinster; National; National City; Northern; Provincial; Royal; and Ulster.

Travellers' cheques can normally be cashed in leading hotels, and at certain travel agencies with facilities for exchange.

CUSTOMS REGULATIONS

United States and Canadian visitors can import into Ireland without payment of duty 2½ lbs. of manufactured tobacco, including cigars and cigarettes; a quarter of a gallon of spirits, including liqueurs and cordials; two-sixths of a gallon of wine; one pint of perfumed spirits; and other dutiable goods to the value of $48 per adult and $12 per child.

Bona-fide personal effects, including clothing, cameras, sports equipment, bicycles and perambulators are also admitted free of duty provided they are not intended as gifts or for sale.

Sporting guns and cartridges can be imported under licence; for conditions see page 59.

There is very little restriction on export. Antiques and paintings carry slight formalities—the store where you make your purchase will help you. Queries can be made at the Export Licence Division, Department of Industry and Commerce, Kildare Street, Dublin (Tel.: 65801).

TRAVEL IN IRELAND

The best way to explore a city is on foot—and the best way to see a country is by road. Probably few would argue with me on the first proposition—many would on the second point. The railways of the world, some profitable, others running at a heavy loss, still have many devotees. For me, it's the road every time. How else can you stop off when something beautiful or intriguing catches your eye—how else find the treasures and surprises that lie off the beaten track? To discover the character of a city, you should tramp. In Dublin, as in any other big city. But here, if you don't like walking, or you happen to feel lazy, you are well looked after by C.I.E. (Coras Iompair Eireann)—Ireland's Transport Company. They publish a useful leaflet called *Discover Dublin by Bus* which lists all the main places of interest in and around the capital, indicates which routes apply to them, and contains a very clear map. Some suggested city tours are included, as well as a list of bus routes serving excursion points further afield. Details are also given of economical "runabout" tickets. For what to see in Dublin, refer to the beginning of Part 3, where I have described the city at length.

Apart from city services, C.I.E. operate extensive coach and rail services, including a number of all-in conducted coach tours. On these, you travel in big, comfortable Worldmaster vehicles with friendly couriers keeping you well-informed and looking after your comfort throughout the journeys. The six to twelve-day tours are in the loveliest parts of Ireland. They operate from Dublin and from Shannon Airport, you stay in first-class hotels all the way, and rates cover the cost of accommodation, meals and tips.

You can also take day or half-day trips from Dublin and other centres, either by road or rail. "Radio Train" excursions are run from Dublin to Galway and Killarney, with musical programmes and broadcast commentary *en route*.

A most economical way of seeing the country is by taking a rail or combined rail-and-road "rambler" ticket on which, for from $14.40 to $26.40, you can travel with absolute freedom over the entire rail and provincial bus system for 15 days. These tickets can be obtained from travel agents or any Irish railway station. C.I.E. also give up to 10 per cent. reductions for "one-way" and "circular" tour arrangements by normal scheduled services, and there are special rates for group travel. A special low cost "explorer" tour of the lesser-known beauty spots is also provided by C.I.E.

C.I.E. offer other services, too. Among these are chauffeur-driven limousine tours from Dublin; limousine golf tours; cruises on the Shannon river and its lakes; steamer trips to the Aran Islands, 30 miles off Galway; and various all-in "package" holidays, enabling you to spend part of your time touring and part at a resort for a few days.

Other suggestions, for tours by private or hire car—

or public transport in some cases over a longer period—include a seven-day tour for book-lovers, "a journey through places rich in literary association, places where great men have thought or written and have therefore inevitably left something of themselves"; a nine-day tour of Ireland's Holy Places, a ten-day tour of antiquities, and a ten-day tour for American visitors. This last pinpoints places of special interest to them, and is best made by car.

A number of British coach companies operate tours in Ireland. These are listed in the Appendices.

INLAND WATERWAYS AND CRUISES

Irish inland waterways are accessible from the sea through the ports of Dublin, Waterford and Limerick. The Grand Canal and the Barrow Navigation are owned and controlled by C.I.E. and visitors who wish to travel on them are required to complete Indemnity Forms, obtainable from C.I.E., Canal Section, James Street Harbour, Dublin, and Canal Office, Shannon Harbour, County Offaly. The River Shannon is controlled by the Shannon Navigation Office, Limerick.

Waterways shown on the map (see page 70) are navigable up to the limits indicated below:

The Grand Canal and Barrow Navigation

   There is a charge of 15 c. per lock

Ringsend Branch—8 locks—Portobello to Sea
 Lock inclusive, falling from the junction to
 the River Liffey .. .. 3m. 6f.
Main Line—1st to 18th lock, rising from Dublin
 to the summit level at Lowtown .. .. 26m. 6f.
Shannon Line—19th to 36th lock, falling from
 summit level at Lowtown to Shannon Harbour, where it joins the Shannon River .. 53m. 3f.

Barrow Line—20th to 28th lock, falling from
  junction at Lowtown to Horse Bridge, Athy,
  where it joins the Barrow Navigation .. 28m. 4f.
River Barrow Navigation—23 locks, falling from
  Horse Bridge, Athy, to Tidal Section at St.
  Mullins .. .. 41m. 3f.
Tidal Section—St. Mullins to Waterford Quay 30m. 0f.

Other lakes and rivers, in many cases, can be navigated
by trailer-drawn vessels, or by canoes. In such cases,
helpful advice will be gladly given by the Honorary Secretary, Athlone Branch, Inland Waterways Association of
Ireland, Royal Hotel, Athlone. If you do not intend taking
your own boat, he will also provide a list of firms with
craft for hire. Two such firms are Shannon Cruisers Ltd.,
Cootehall, Boyle, Co. Roscommon and Joy Line Cruisers,
18 Berkeley Street, Dublin 7 (Tel.: 43121). The latter is
the only company operating on the Grand Canal and
starting its cruises at Lucan, eleven miles from Dublin.
By starting there, you avoid the series of closely situated
locks near the city end, and from Lucan onwards the locks
are spaced widely enough not to cause hindrance. Over one
part of this waterway, there is no lock for over twenty miles.
However, most river enthusiasts will agree that where locks
are fairly frequent, they provide welcome and interesting
breaks in the journey.

At the summit level of the Grand Canal beyond Roberts-
town, you can either carry straight on to the Shannon or
branch southwards to meet the Barrow at Athy and then
go on to Carlow. South of Carlow, the canal presents
some difficulties for the novice, and the Joy Line Company
do not allow their craft beyond the town. The canal proper
is in good repair, the locks are easy to work and the lock-
keepers are helpful. You are never far from towns and
villages where you can obtain refreshments or supplies.

From the twelfth lock at Lucan to Shannon Harbour, the distance is 70 miles; from there (near Banagher) to Athlone it is 21 miles. From Athlone, it is 49 miles to Carrick-on-Shannon, 60 miles to Boyle, the same distance to Killaloe, and 35 miles to Rooskey. The latter, as well as Banagher, Lanesboro and Portumna, are villages worth visiting. Water-skiing championships are held every year at Killaloe. And of course, there is plenty of fishing on a journey of this kind!

River Shannon Navigation extends from Limerick to Lough Key on the Boyle river, a distance of 130 miles, and includes the tidal lock at Ardnacrusha as well as six other locks. Above Carrick-on-Shannon, there are alternative routes. One branches right to Leitrim and Battlebridge, a distance of $5\frac{1}{2}$ miles. The other, more popular route is up the Boyle river to Lough Key, a distance of 9 miles. Cabin cruisers with one dinghy are charged 40 c. per lock, rowboats and canoes are charged 12 c. per lock. A pass to cover the complete navigation from Limerick to the Northern Limits is obtainable from the Shannon Navigation Office at Limerick, Athlone or Knockvicar, at a cost of $1.60. All the bridges on the Shannon, with two exceptions only, have a clearance of 15 feet 6 inches at normal summer level. The exceptions are Portumna (8 feet) and Rooskey (11 feet) which are swing bridges and will be opened on request, at a charge of 40 c. Navigable depths vary. The ideal draught is 3 feet 6 inches, but if handled with care in the shallower reaches, boats with draught up to 5 feet can navigate the river successfully. The limiting factor of navigation on the Shannon is the Ardnacrusha Lock— 105 feet long and 19 feet 6 inches wide. Passage through the locks is permitted between sunrise and sunset, Monday to Saturday. At any other time, and on Sundays, advance arrangements should be made with the lock-keeper concerned.

Seagoing vessels arriving in the Shannon Estuary from the Atlantic are advised to pick up a pilot at Scattery Island, to bring them as far as Limerick Docks. A river pilot should also be engaged to navigate the vessel from Limerick to Killaloe, from where the owner can navigate although, because of existing shoals, a set of charts is essential. These are available from the I.W.A.I. at the address given above.

Further information can be obtained from the I.W.A.I. or from the Irish Charter Boat Association, 18 Berkeley Street, Dublin, 7. An especially comfortable cruising holiday can be made on a luxuriously appointed motor vessel operated by Irish River Floatels Ltd. on the Shannon. This can be booked through Frames Tours, Ltd., 25–31 Tavistock Place, London, W.C.1 (Tel.: EUSton 3488).

Visitors are always welcome to join the Shannon Boat Rally, which takes place annually. Details are obtainable from Cynthia Rice, Hon. Secretary, Shannon Boat Rally, I.W.A.I., Coosan Point, Athlone.

The Athlone Branch of the I.W.A.I. also publishes a very useful book of charts for the River Shannon. It costs six shillings.

CANOE CAMPING HOLIDAYS

Matt Murphy Enterprises (Ballymaquirk, Banteer, Co. Cork) organises canoe-camping holidays on the Black-water River, which flows over 90 miles from a point near Ballydesmond, through wonderful country to the Atlantic at Youghal. Canoeing is downstream, and the river is ideal for beginners. Canoeing or camping experience are unnecessary. (Life jackets are supplied!) Everyone helps with the chores, but meals are provided and cooked by party leaders from Matt Murphy Enterprises. Fresh food is served at all times, not the tinned variety. You sleep in a tent, shared with one other person. There is free trout and coarse fishing on the river. A day can be spent caving at Rosken on the banks of the Blackwater.

Although the complete river itinerary takes 14 days, parties can start and finish a week's holiday anywhere they wish, but these shorter tours usually commence at Rathcool and finish at Killavullen, or begin at Killavullen and end at Lismore. The cost for one week is $22.70 and for two weeks $44.40. Large groups may like to note that one adult can go free with every ten paying persons. The charges include the use of all equipment, everything necessary being supplied—canoe accessories, tent and groundsheet, sleeping bag and sheet, anorak, eating utensils and air bed. All you need are your own towels. Also inclusive are three meals daily, and the services of the party leaders; the rail/sea fares to the River Blackwater from your home town via Fishguard, Glasgow or Liverpool. All-in costs from London, Manchester, Cardiff and Belfast can also be quoted. Parties are met on arrival at the railway station.

Rigid type self-hire canoes are also available from Matt Murphy Enterprises.

HORSE-DRAWN CARAVAN HOLIDAYS

Galleon Holidays (Head Office: Eccleston Court, Gillingham Street, London, S.W.1) arrange holiday "cruises" in horse-drawn, Romany-type caravans—an absolutely unique way of travelling, and certainly a leisurely, peaceful one. You "cruise" in County Kerry, taking in Glengarriff, Killarney, and Blarney Castle and you can fly or go by rail/sea to Cork—the caravan site is nearby.

The all-in cost is $108.60 by air (14 days) or $105.60 by rail/sea (16 days). These charges include berth reservation

1. An Aer Lingus car ferry aircraft

2. River Liffey and Dublin quays

3. Powerscourt Waterfall, near Enniskerry

4. Glendaloch, Co. Wicklow

in a 4-berth caravan, breakfast, lunch, high tea and evening tea and biscuits from lunch on the day of arrival until after breakfast on the day of departure; travel tickets whether by air or rail/sea and in the latter case, reserved berths on steamers in both directions, as well as reserved seats on trains outside Ireland; the transfers from Cork to the caravan site; services of the tour leader, of mobile canteen and staff, also tips.

Accommodation is in Romany-type, canvas-covered 4-berth caravans (two upper and two lower) with Dunlopillo mattresses, washbasins, small cooking stove with calor gas for heating and lighting, locker storage for clothes. Married couples should note that wives are accommodated in a ladies' caravan, husbands in one for men. Families of four can have exclusive use of a caravan. The mobile canteen goes ahead of the caravans and prepares meals in advance. The cooker in each caravan enables occupants to make their own tea when they wish. One horse is provided for each of the caravans, driven by the occupants. The tour leader, an experienced Irish guide, stays with the party throughout the tour, looks after and feeds the horses and arranges entertainment for caravanners.

Anything from 10 to 20 miles may be covered each day, some days being left free. Wayside, lakeside and seaside picnics are arranged. Villagers and townsfolk *en route* welcome the caravan parties and usually invite them to join in music, dancing and other local entertainment. Also excursions are made to castles and other places of historical interest, as well as villages and farms. Obviously, anyone going on a holiday of this type must be prepared to assist with chores to some extent.

Matt Murphy Enterprises, Ballymaquirk, Banteer, Co. Cork, also offer this type of holiday, with similar arrangements.

MOTORING

The perfect way of travelling in a country like Ireland is by car. There are 20,000 miles of good, well-signposted roads and, apart from the occasional one in Dublin, traffic jams are unknown. In Ireland, you will have some idea of what our own roads were like in the 'twenties, and even the early 'thirties—and we must hope that Ireland's growing popularity will not alter these conditions too rapidly. For the moment, fortunately, we can drive, as leisurely as we please, on the left as at home, put on an occasional spurt when we feel like it, and at no time suffer from motorway-itis or narrow-lane cramp by being bowled along or held static by hordes of other road-users. As the Irish Tourist Board says in one of its booklets: "Here you can discover what a car is really for!"

The Board issues two excellent booklets on touring. Both include details of the conducted coach tours mentioned in the previous section, but they are chiefly designed for motorists. One contains itineraries for Dublin and the East Coast; Killarney and the South-West; Galway and the West; Donegal and the Yeats Country; also a "Grand Scenic Tour" and Through Routes. In the other booklet, which also covers bus and rail tours, there are motoring itineraries from Shannon Airport and Cobh to Dublin (from 3–7 days); Circular Motoring Tours in various parts of the country (from 5–7 days); and details of the specialised tours I mentioned in the previous section.

Routes given in the first booklet can be followed from the road map issued by the Board. It has a scale of 12 miles to the inch and costs 1s. (12 cents). If you prefer more detail, Ordnance Survey maps with half-inch or quarter-inch scale can be bought at Irish Tourist Offices in Ireland and at most stationers. The first of these is available in twenty-five sheets, the second in five sheets. Another series is on the scale of one inch to a mile, and has a corresponding set of geological survey maps. There are also maps on the scale of six inches to the mile and twenty-five inches to the mile, but these are hardly suitable for the normal motoring tour. Large-scale plans of towns can also be obtained. Maps of Northern Ireland are issued by the Ordnance Survey Department of that territory, in Belfast.

I have given details of the air and sea ferries under "How To Get There", and this section also indicates the documents which motorists require on leaving Britain. To enter Ireland, you also need a Temporary Importation Permit, obtainable (free) either on arrival or beforehand through your motoring organisation. Incidentally, the AA have offices in Dublin (23 Suffolk Street), Cork (5 South Mall) and Belfast (5 Oxford Street). The RAC have an office in Belfast at 65 Chichester Street; and the Royal Irish Automobile Club are at 34 Dawson Street, Dublin and 55 South Mall, Cork.

CAR HIRE

If you do not take your own car, a large number of hire firms is at your disposal in Dublin, Cork, Limerick and most of the larger towns. Arrangements can be made for a car to await your arrival at airport, seaport or station, and, at the end of your holiday, it will be collected from your departure point. Daily or weekly hire rates vary according to the size and make of the car but, for example, in the off-season, a Ford Anglia or a Volkswagen can be hired for as little as $24 a week, *including free unlimited mileage*. The same cars would cost an average of $43 in July or August.

Although some hire firms have one or two "bonded" cars, you cannot take non-bonded hire cars from Eire into

Northern Ireland. If you are continuing your holiday in the north, you will need to arrange for a car from that area to meet you at the border, if you still want one. (This only applies to Eire hire cars. You are free to cross the border to Eire in a Northern Ireland hire car; and in either direction with your own car, when the initial set of documents held on arrival in either territory is sufficient for both.)

Firms like Dan Ryan, Joe Malone, Bolands, Murray's, and Joe Cahill, are among the well-known hire specialists a list of whom is obtainable from the Tourist Board Offices—for addresses see the Appendices. Joe Malone offers visitors an "Auto-Package" holiday which includes the hire of the self-drive car and the hotel accommodation from $37.80 weekly in the off-peak period. These holidays can commence in Dublin, Cork or Limerick.

Ryans (as distinct from Dan Ryan) provide the self-drive motoring end of a 15-day inclusive "Air-Auto" Tour, linked with Aer Lingus and BEA. These tours are not rigidly planned—special itineraries can be arranged to suit individual tastes. Ask Ryans for their leaflet on the subject.

* * *

Whether in your own or a hire car, you will enjoy driving in lovely country unspoiled by industrial smoke and clutter, or by much heavy traffic, as most supplies go by rail. Petrol supplies are easily obtainable. Directional information, milages and warnings are clearly marked on signposts, although some bends are unmarked. The name of every town and village is shown on its outskirts, and as you leave each one, you will find that the next place on your route is indicated. You are unlikely to get lost, but if any problem arises, all you have to do in "Ireland of the Welcomes" is ask the first person you meet for help. Your reward will be greater than it could be anywhere else—except in heaven, which, along with the earth, all the Irish are prepared to move for you.

One thing they cannot or seem unable to do is prevent dogs running out dangerously close and barking at cars. This occurs frequently and if it happens to you, just slow down a bit, but do not change course, and all will be well. Worrisome though it is to you, the dog knows what it is doing.

CARAVANS

Caravans can be parked at special sites in the bigger resorts (the average rate is 30 c. a night). In some cases, caravans can be hired on the sites, and there are numerous firms offering caravans for touring at $15.12–$25.20 weekly. A list of these is available from Irish Tourist Offices. You can also obtain a list of firms from the Irish Caravan Council, 77 Lower Leeson Street, Dublin. Their member-firms conform to high standards designed to protect hirers.

Apart from recognised camping sites, you can usually park anywhere you like in Ireland, so long as you ask permission.

Under Travel in Ireland, I have mentioned the firms which offer unusual, "off-beat" holidays in horse-drawn, Romany-type caravans.

MOTORISED CARAVANS

Auto Caravan Self-Drive, Ltd. (Curran House, 12 Fleet Street, Dublin, Tel.: 79512) has self-drive motorised caravans for hire—as distinct from the kind you need to tow. The vehicles are converted Volkswagen and Ford Thames Station Wagons, available in 2-, 4- or 6-berth models.

Standard equipment includes 2-ring gas cooker with

grill; 7–10-gallon water supply; fitted curtains; tiled floors; wardrobes, drawers, tables and Dunlopillo upholstery. The interior has seating and dining accommodation by day, becomes a bedroom at night. Bedding is supplied if required at an extra charge of $1.20 per person per week. Roof racks are fitted free of charge.

The weekly unlimited rates, not including cost of petrol, of course, are: (2-berth) $79; (4-berth) $93.50; (6-berth) $130. These are summer season rates, applicable from 15th May until 30th September. There are considerable reductions for the rest of the year. The firm also provides a normal self-drive car hire service, with vehicles ranging from Austin Mini to Ford Zephyr.

It should be noted that no vehicles hired in Eire can pass into Northern Ireland. This is a British Customs regulation.

Obvious advantages of a motorised caravan are that it dispenses with towing, hotel and—to some extent—parking problems, makes timetables unnecessary, and is ideal for families with children whose enjoyment need not be restricted as it can be under other conditions.

CLIMATE

I suppose I am sticking my neck out when I say that if it rains in Ireland, it soon clears again. Well, not always, but quite often. This has to be said about a country with a high rainfall—because frankly, when in Ireland, I am so content that I don't really worry about the weather.

What matters is the beauty and the peace. Anyway, the Irish winters are mild, the summers cool. July and August, of course, are the warmest months, with temperatures averaging between 58 and 60 degrees Fahrenheit. February is the coldest, down between 40 and 42 degrees Fahrenheit.

The sunniest month is June, and May—especially in the north, west and midlands—is a good runner-up.

The highest rainfalls occur in the mountain areas. Also, rainfall is greater in the west than in the east. Except in the mountains, snow rarely occurs, and is very slight when it does.

LANGUAGE

Apart from a few remote places, mainly along the west coast, English is spoken and understood throughout the country, and the majority of official notices are posted bilingually. During the last century, the English forbade the teaching of Irish in schools, even in the west, and use of the language declined rapidly. Efforts to revive it were made by the Gaelic League founded in 1893 and inspired by Dr. Douglas Hyde, later Eire's first President. Irish is now widely used in the western counties, is the official language of the state, and is taught in all schools, English being a secondary subject in many of them.

Even in the areas where Irish is used extensively, you will notice that if you happen to be in a group of local people, they will speak English in order not to offend you. The Irish brogue—the accent with which English is spoken—was evident at court in the time of the Tudors. My fellow travel writer, the late Gordon Cooper, remarked on the fact that in the 1623 Folio edition of Shakespeare's plays, many words are spelt as they are pronounced in Ireland today. A beast is a "baste" and a murderer is a "murtherer" and other "brogue spellings" in that edition are "discoorse", "hoord", "rayson", and "retrait". As Cooper said: "It is interesting to think that were Shakespeare to return to earth today he would probably have to go to Dublin in order to understand his own plays."

WHERE TO STAY

The Irish Tourist Board gives all hotels and guesthouses an official grading according to the facilities and degree of luxury offered to visitors. There is also a fixed maximum price for each place, applied to overnight, daily or weekly stay, and to meals.

Hotels in the "A" Category, with a star, are graded as first-class for cuisine and service. "A" hotels and guesthouses without the star have a high standard of cuisine and service, with h. and c. in all bedrooms. "B" establishments are well-furnished and comfortable, hotels having h. and c. in most bedrooms, guesthouses in some. "B/C" and "C" establishments offer well-kept comfortable accommodation with h. and c. in some bedrooms. "D" premises are clean and comfortable, but have limited facilities.

All these places are in the Board's Official List of Hotels and Guesthouses, with full details of facilities and prices. A supplementary list is issued of approved boarding house accommodation in Dublin, Skerries, Dun Laoghaire, Bray, Arklow, Greystones, Tramore, Cork City and the West Cork area; Killarney, the Dingle Peninsula, Ballybunion, Kilkee, Galway City and Salthill, Achill Island, Bundoran, Buncrana and Moville, Greencastle. Farm houses where similar accommodation can be found are also in this list. These lists are freely available from the Board. So is one giving supplementary accommodation in coarse fishing and sea angling centres—specially approved for anglers.

Advance booking is recommended, especially for July and August, and you can make reservations directly with the hotel or guesthouse, or through your travel agent. In emergency, if you arrive without having booked in advance, you will find that the Irish Tourist Offices in Dublin, Cork,

Galway, Killarney and Sligo operate a "Bed Bureau" for accommodation in their areas. This is a free service. You have to pay only for the telephone calls.

The Northern Ireland Tourist Board also issues a list of approved accommodation.

Throughout the touring section of this book (Parts 3 and 4) many hotels are described—in most cases, with my personal recommendation. But wherever you go in Ireland you are very unlikely to be disappointed with the places in which you stay.

The well-known *Farm Holiday Guide*, published at 18 High Street, Paisley, Scotland, contains a seven-page section on Ireland.

HOTEL RATES, 1968

Grade	Single Room From	To	Double Room From	To	*Daily (per person) From	To	Private Bath (per person) From	To
A*	$3.00	$11.40	$6.00	$17.10	$5.00	$17.10	$1.20	$2.40
A	2.40	3.90	4.80	7.80	4.75	8.40	.90	1.50
B	2.00	3.90	3.95	7.80	4.50	8.10	.70	1.50
B/C	1.90	3.60	3.00	7.20	3.60	6.15	.60	1.20
C	1.50	3.60	2.90	4.80	3.00	5.30	.60	.85
D	1.20	1.80	2.40	3.60	2.70	4.00	—	—

*For not less than 3 days

FOOD AND DRINK

The food in Ireland is very similar to our own—the only difference being that its flavour depends more on the high quality of ingredients in what is served than on the special sauces and seasonings typical of Continental catering.

41

Also, as at home, you have a normal-sized breakfast. In short, apart from a tendency in some places to overcook meat that we like rare, Irish food is very good indeed, as I have emphasised in the descriptions of various places mentioned in Parts 3 and 4. Lunch in an average hotel or restaurant costs from 72 c. to $1.15. High tea, consisting of a mixed grill with chips, tea, bread-and-butter, costs from 80 c. to $1.25.

Scotch whisky costs 32 c. a measure, Irish whiskey 28 c. —bear in mind that Irish spirit measures are much more generous than ours, there being eight measures to the pint. Brandy is 45 c., Irish gin 28 c. for the same measure. Sherry is 25 c. a glass. Draught stout and ale are 23 c. a pint; bottled stout, ale, lager and cider are priced between 14 c. and 21 c. a half-pint. These are normal bar prices— you will pay a little more, of course, in lounge and cocktail bars.

Apart from the restaurants in the hotels I have mentioned in Parts 3 and 4, there are many other good restaurants. In Dublin, for instance, these include the *Bailey* and the *Red Bank* for seafood; *Jammets* for French cuisine; the *Unicorn, Quo Vadis* and *Bernardo* for Italian food and steaks; the *Golden Orient* Indian restaurant; the *Dolphin* and the *Metropole Grill*. The main restaurant at the airport also serves first-class food, and other places out of town are *Haddington House*, Dun Laoghaire; *Shangri La* and the *Guinea Pig*, Dalkey; the *Abbey Tavern* at Howth, for seafood. The following is an additional list of recommended restaurants in places I have described around the country.

CORK CITY	Buffet Grill
	Guinness Restaurant
	Oyster Grill
	Vienna Woods
	Intercontinental Hotel

42

CO. CORK	Ballylickey House, Bantry
	Shorecliffe House, Glandore
	Casey's Hotel, Glengarriff
	West Cork Hotel, Skibbereen
	The Haven, Schull
	Airport Restaurant
CO. CLARE	Shannon Airport Restaurant
	Aberdeen Arms, Lahinch (Seafood)
	The Falls, Ennistymon
CO. DONEGAL	Drumbeg Hotel, Inver
	Carrigart Hotel, Carrigart
	Maghery House, Bundoran
	Tullaghan House, near Bundoran
CO. GALWAY	Lydon's Restaurant, Galway City
	Twelve Bens, Barna
	Sweeney's Hotel, Oughterard
	Renvyle House, Renvyle
	Leenane Hotel, Leenane
	Paddy Burke's, Clarenbridge
	Glynn's Hotel, Gort
CO. KERRY	Glenbeigh Hotel, Glenbeigh
	Towers Hotel, Glenbeigh
	Ross Hotel, Killarney
	Hotel Europe, Killarney
	International Hotel, Killarney
	Ardna Shide Guest House, Caragh Lake
	Southern Lake Hotel, Waterville
	Benner's Hotel, Tralee
CO. LIMERICK	Brazen Head, Limerick,
	Dunraven Arms, Adare
CO. LOUTH	Derryhale Hotel, Dundalk
CO. MAYO	Old Head Hotel, Louisburgh
	Breaffey House Hotel, Castlebar
	Newport House, Newport
CO. SLIGO	Silver Grill, Sligo
CO. TIPPERARY	Cashel Palace Hotel, Cashel
	Cahir House Hotel, Cahir
	Kilcoran Lodge, Cahir

CO. TIPPERARY	Ormond Hotel, Nenagh
(*cont.*)	O'Meara's Hotel, Nenagh
CO. CAVAN	The Park Hotel, Virginia
CO. WEXFORD	Strand Hotel, Rosslare
CO. WICKLOW	Glenview Hotel, Glen of the Downs
	Wicklow Hills, Roundwood
	Glencormac Hotel, Kilmacanogue
	Royal Hotel, Bray
CO. MEATH	Headford Arms, Kells
	Aclare House, Drumconrath
CO. WESTMEATH	Shamrock Lodge, Athlone
	Prince of Wales Hotel, Athlone
	Bon-Bon, Athlone
CO. LEIX	Egan's Restaurant, Portlaois
CO. WATERFORD	Tower Hotel, Waterford
	The Haven, Dunmore East
CO. LEITRIM	Bush Hotel, Carrick-on-Shannon

Soda Bread

If the convenience of sliced, wrapped and frequently tasteless bread impresses you less than the farmhouse flavour of good wheaten baking, you will love the Irish soda bread which is served at every meal; a natural bread, without any make-up. I usually bring a load back with me when I go there, but unfortunately one cannot keep hopping over, and for those who like soda bread and do-it-yourself baking sufficiently, here is the recipe:

Ingredients:

1 lb. of white or brown flour
1 Tspnfl of bread soda
1 Tspnfl Bex Tartar
½ Pint of buttermilk
Pinch of salt

44

Sieve the dry ingredients into a bowl and add the butter-milk. Mix to a fairly soft dough. Bake in moderate oven (350°) for 45 minutes.

Irish Coffee

Irish Coffee, say the Irish, is "the most delectable drink that has ever crossed the palate". They also insist that it cannot be made properly with anything but their whiskey. The ingredients are cream ("rich as an Irish brogue"), coffee ("strong as a friendly hand"), sugar ("sweet as the tongue of a rogue"), whiskey ("smooth as the wit of the land").

To prepare the brew, heat a stemmed whiskey goblet. Pour in a jigger of Irish Whiskey, "the only whiskey with the smooth taste and full body needed," add three cubes of sugar. Fill the goblet with strong black coffee to within one inch of the brim. Stir to dissolve the sugar. Top off to the brim with whipped cream slightly aerated, so that the cream floats on top. Do NOT stir after adding the cream, as the true flavour is obtained by drinking the hot coffee and Irish whiskey through the cream. For convenience while you are on the move, you can also buy Irish Coffee chocolate, which is very good, too, but the effect is certainly not the same. If the Irish police ever use breathalysers, this could cause some problems!

SHOPPING

Ireland is internationally famed for its tweeds and linen and the glass that comes from Waterford. These are all very good buys in a country where a lot of thought is given to quality of both merchandise and service.

As designers like Sybil Connolly have done a great deal to make Dublin a new centre of high fashion in the last few years, female visitors will be looking for something special to bring home with them. This can be found in Kay Petersen's shop, Anna Livia, in Dawson Street where, in a boutique much praised by *Harper's Bazaar* and other important publications, there are stylish coats and suits made not merely of those wonderful tweeds but also in brilliant contemporary colours. Donegal tweeds are also on sale here, as well as tweed hats, separates in handwoven wool and cotton, pure wool lightweight shirts and shifts, mohair and other sweaters, with matching slacks for après-ski wear; evening separates and evening dresses in Irish wool lace. This is one of the places for which allowance should be made when drawing currency from the bank prior to departure. So is the Richard Alan Shop, where the well-known Jack Clarke range is available.

Tweed suits, coats and handknit goods can be bought, too, at Creation Boutique in Duke Street. Nearby are two leading department stores—Brown Thomas & Co. Ltd. and the House of Switzer—both with a wide range of goods on sale.

Among the words we have won from the French, "souvenirs" is perhaps the only one which conjures up thoughts of something less attractive than its sound. We cannot blame the French alone, for in every tourist country, including theirs and ours, the word has long been associated with the most dreadful commercial "tat" and although shops selling tat can be spotted a mile away and avoided, the label still gets fixed to those selling quality goods, and I wish a new word could be found for the latter. Until one is, I am always willing to chat around the subject before getting to the point, or rather the place I want to draw to readers' attention!

In this case, I am thinking of Fergus O'Farrell's splendid shop in Duke Street. He specialises in high grade handmade items, including fanciful figures out of Ireland's past, carved and beautifully finished in fine woods. His leaflet describing some twenty of these figures contains historical and amusing notes. About St. Patrick, the patron Saint of Ireland, who was not an Irishman, but is loved by Irishmen all over the world, he says: "Some learned men are putting forward the theory (almost heretical) that there was more than one Patrick, possibly three. This notion is most upsetting to the good Saint himself and he is worried in case he didn't exist." His image comes in two sizes and works out at £2 10s. ($6) and £1 1s. ($2.50). And in true Irish fashion, Mr. O'Farrell caters for both worlds by offering charming angels and devils for sale. You can also buy many other handwoven and wrought iron items here, and, if you are a member, charge your purchases to your account with the Diners' Club.

Hand-made figures in wood, Irish porcelain and ceramics are obtainable, too, as well as Waterford crystal, at Robert Smyth & Sons Ltd. on St. Stephen's Green. The Tourist Board publish a list of shops at which you can buy a great variety of goods, including Aran knitwear, Celtic illumination and calligraphy, Connemara marble, Donegal carpets, copper ware, Crios and Crios caps and mats, curraghs, dolls, Irish linen and crochet, pictures, plaques, pottery, shillelagh brooches and keyrings. It also tells you where to buy a leprechaun—made of felt, plaster, nickel, shell or pottery.

Many hotels, including those in the excellent Great Southern group, have shops in or close to the foyer, selling a wide range of craft items and other "souvenirs".

You can also buy goods in the duty-free shop at Shannon International Airport, where products from many European countries are displayed. The Irish goods shown include Donegal tweeds, Waterford crystal, Belleek china, Armagh porcelain, Kilkenny pottery, linen and Aran knitwear.

47

The Desmond Kenny "souvenir" shop in Galway is another of the places at which you can use your Diners' Club Credit Card. If you do not have one of these useful "passports" look into the scope it offers you abroad by writing to the head office of the club, at 214 Oxford Street, London, W.1. American readers will know that the New York Office is at 10 Columbus Circle, and there are other offices in Los Angeles, Chicago, San Francisco, Pittsburgh, Honolulu, Miami Beach and Toronto. The card can be used also for credit at a great many hotels and restaurants, and for car hire, too.

BEACHES AND BATHING

Along the Irish coast there are countless uncrowded, sandy beaches, many of which offer good locations for safe bathing. I have referred to a large number of them in the touring section of the book (Parts 3 and 4) but the following is a regional ready-reference list which you may find useful. Unless otherwise indicated, all are at places where there is at least one hotel or guest house, details of which can be obtained from the Irish Tourist Board offices in London, Birmingham, Manchester and Glasgow, or from your travel agent when booking passage.

CO. DUBLIN	Balbriggan
	Malahide
	Portmarnock
	Dalkey (bathing in rock coves)
	Killiney
CO. LOUTH	Blackrock
CO. MEATH	Bettystown ⎫ Twin villages connected
	Laytown ⎭ by beach, dunes
CO. WICKLOW	Greystones
	Wicklow
	Brittas Bay

CO. WEXFORD	Ballymoney (no accommodation)
	Cahore (no accommodation)
	Curracloe
	Fethard-on-Sea (no accommodation)
	Duncannon
CO. WATERFORD	Clonlea
	Dungarvan
	Ardmore
CO. CORK	Garryvoe
	Ballycotton (bathing in coves)
	Cobh (some bathing nearby)
	Crosshaven
	Myrtleville
	Oysterhaven (accommodation but no hotels)
	Garrettstown
	Courtmacsherry
	Rosscarbery
	Schull (coastal village—bathing)
	Kilcrohane
	Bantry (beaches and coves nearby)
CO. KERRY	Inch
	Dingle (bathing nearby)
	Dunquin (no accommodation)
	Cloghane (no accommodation)
	Castlegregory (no accommodation)
	Tralee (beaches nearby)
	Kenmare (bathing in coves)
	Castlecove
	Waterville
	Ballinskelligs
	Ballyheigue
CO. GALWAY	Spiddal (no accommodation)
	Roundstone
	Clifden
	Renvyle
CO. MAYO	Louisburgh (beaches nearby)
	Newport
	Mallarany

CO. SLIGO	Enniscrone
	Strandhill
	Rosses Point
	Mullaghmore
CO. DONEGAL	Rossnowlagh
	Inver
	Killybegs (beach nearby)
	Malinmore
	Rosbeg
	Narin ⎱ Twin villages with beach
	Portnoo ⎰
	Burtonport (no accommodation)
	Bunnbeg
	Port-na-blagh
	Dunfanaghy
	Rosapenna
	Downings
	Carrigart
	Rathmullan (beach on Lough Swilly)
	Buncrana
	Clonmany (beaches nearby)
	Ballyliffin
	Greencastle
	Moville (shingle beach, sandy coves)

NORTHERN IRELAND

With the exception of Groomsport, the following places with beach and bathing facilities also have accommodation—at least one guest house or hotel. As in the case of Eire, some places listed are developed resorts.

CO. DOWN	Annalong
	Ballywalter
	Bangor
	Donaghadee
	Dundrum
	Groomsport
	Killinchy
	Holywood

CO. DOWN	Kilkeel
(cont.)	Newcastle
	Portaferry
	Rostrevor
	Warrenpoint
CO. ANTRIM	Ballintoy
	Ballycastle
	Carnlough
	Carrickfergus
	Cushendall
	Cushendun
	Giant's Causeway
	Glenarm
	Larne
	Portballintrae
	Portrush
	Whitehead
CO. LONDONDERRY	Castlerock
	Downhill
	Portstewart

CAMPING

Although the weather in Ireland is not exactly ideal for this kind of holiday, many people do go camping. There are many recognised camping sites, but you can usually camp wherever you like, so long as you ask for permission.

An unusual type of camping holiday, less subject to the vagaries of the weather, is offered by C.I.E., Ireland's Transport Company. They have a number of railway carriages which have been converted into camping coaches—virtually seaside cottages—available at Dungarvan, Killarney and Youghal. These provide spacious accommodation for eight people, a living room and a kitchen. The coaches are fully equipped with lighting, heating, running water, gas cooker and cooking utensils, crockery, cutlery, bed-linen and blankets.

51

Coach rentals range from $19 a week in the off-season to $34 a week at peak. During your stay, you can obtain and use a special holiday "runabout" ticket for travel by rail or bus within a 50-mile radius of the coach. There is only one condition of hire—that coach users purchase in advance three adult rail return tickets from their home stations (two children counting as one adult). This type of holiday can be booked through your travel agent, or the Passenger Sales Manager, C.I.E., 59 Upper O'Connell Street, Dublin.

At Dungarvan you can bathe, play on a 9-hole golf course, or go trout fishing in the River Colligan. Killarney speaks for itself, but see what I have said about it in Part 3. Youghal has a good beach, golfing, boating and sea-fishing facilities.

HOLIDAY ART COURSES

For several years a most successful Holiday School of Art has been directed by Kenneth Webb whose work, well-known in Ireland, has also gained recognition in England and America. He has lectured extensively in England, and appeared in a series of television programmes. Through years of experience as an art college teacher, he has developed a teaching technique which is especially suited to the amateur. His method is to give detailed explanation with a demonstration in oil, watercolour or gouache at every sketching site, and then follow through with personal attention.

The centre for each season's course is chosen for its variety of sketching sites and its climate. The weather in south and western Ireland is milder than in England—consequently it is most suitable for the courses, and usually allows for a full outdoor programme, although a working studio is also available at all times. While the School has drawn students from all over Europe, the United States, Canada, South Africa and India, each is encouraged to

52

develop an individual style, and because this involves strict limitation of numbers, early booking is essential.

Sketching sites, of course, are chosen in many beautiful areas, and students can take part in either residential, non-residential or vocational courses. The residential courses are accommodated in comfortable hotels which are registered with the Irish Tourist Board, single rooms, although plentiful, having to be booked early and costing a guinea extra. Fees range from $35.30 to $39 per week, and are inclusive of all main meals, accommodation, tuition, lectures, demonstrations and car transport between the hotel and the sketching site. Payment has to be made one week before the course commences. Non-painting friends can be accommodated with the sketching party at a reduced fee.

The fee for non-residential courses is $14.80 weekly, payable when booking, or $3.60 a day for part-time students. This fee does not cover meals and accommodation—there is a wide range of hotels and guest-houses from which to choose. (See under Where to Stay.)

Exhibitions of students' work are held in Ireland, Britain and the United States. Many students have sold their paintings at professional prices.

Lectures are held during the evenings, covering art appreciation, history of art, contemporary design, etc., and these are illustrated with colour slides. Programmes are sent to students shortly before the course begins. Materials are on sale at the studio, although large items have to be ordered in advance. Easels and stools can be hired in advance.

Vocational courses are designed mainly for the younger student and special facilities are available for all art examinations. Beginners are particularly welcome. Bathing, tennis and other recreations are available.

53

The School has a permanent home at Ballywalter, a quiet fishing village 22 miles from Belfast. A studio built in 1963 gives a fine view of the coast and private access to the beach. If they wish, students can camp on grass between the beach and studio, screened from the latter.

There is about 400 square feet of studio space and plenty of room on the lawns outside. Sketching sites include the Mountains of Mourne, farm buildings, cottages, harbours with boats and trees. Accommodation is available in hotels, guest houses and caravans, at inclusive fees ranging from $25 to $40. The bus service into Belfast is a good one. Other centres for holiday courses include places in the Donegal Highlands, Killarney, Cork (taking in the Blarney Castle and Kinsale Harbour areas) and Roundstone, Connemara.

Courses are planned on a weekly basis, but students often stay for longer periods and visit more than one centre. A reduction of two guineas is given on the third and any subsequent week of a residential booking. Transport can be arranged between the centres, for an extra charge depending on the expense involved. Applications should be made at the earliest possible date to: The Organising Secretary, Mrs. Joan Webb, The Warren Studio, Ballywalter, Newtownards, Co. Down, Northern Ireland (Tel.: Ballywalter 232). It should be noted that the organisers reserve the right to cancel any course for which insufficient bookings are received.

Travel to Ireland can be arranged either through your own or the organisers' travel agents.

ANGLING

Experienced anglers who travel abroad will know that its coastline, rivers, streams and lakes make Ireland very much their kind of country. They will be aware that there is probably no other place in the world where such a great variety of fishing can be enjoyed so easily, in such a small area, so inexpensively. For others who are interested, the following notes may be helpful.

SALMON FISHING

Salmon are found in all the larger rivers, in many of the smaller ones, and in numerous lakes. The best salmon fisheries are preserved and let by the week or month, although day tickets are available for some. Quite a number of fisheries are owned by hotels and these are reserved for their guests. Other waters on which visitors can fish are controlled by angling clubs. On some lakes, notably Lough Corrib, Lough Fern in Donegal, Lough Currane at Waterville, and the Killarney Lakes, there is free fishing. Free salmon fishing is possible, too, on rivers, depending on weather and water conditions. Certain rivers provide salmon fishing in spring; March and April are usually the best months. Among the good spring rivers are the Boyne, Nore, Munster, Blackwater, Slaney and Suir. Spring salmon average 10 to 12 lbs. and in some rivers there are larger fish, from 20 lbs. upwards. Some of the best summer salmon fishing is in the smaller lakes and rivers of Connemara, Donegal and Kerry.

You need a rod licence for salmon fishing. Its cost varies from $2.40 for 7 days to $7.20 for a full season in one fishery district, $9.60 for a full season for all fishery districts.

SEA TROUT FISHING

Sea trout are plentiful in the smaller lakes and rivers around the coastal areas, particularly west Cork, Connemara, Donegal and Kerry. They are found as early as May in some places, but the best months in most waters

are July, August and September. Irish sea trout are not usually large, averaging $\frac{3}{4}$ lb. to 2 lbs.

As in the case of salmon, the best sea trout fisheries are preserved, both by private owners who let them by the month, week or day, and by hotels where the fishing is reserved for guests. Again, too, angling associations control some good sea trout fishing, and there is some free fishing in a number of lakes, including Caragh Lake in Kerry and Lough Currane, Waterville. Coastal streams are free, as are most salt water places where sea trout can be caught. You require a salmon rod licence for sea trout fishing.

BROWN TROUT FISHING

Brown trout are found in all the big lakes and most of the smaller ones. They also occur in every river and stream. Those of the coastal regions mentioned above are usually small. Bigger fish can be found in the limestone lakes of the central plain, especially Arrow, Carra, Derravaragh, Ennell and Owel. In these waters the average weight is 2 lbs. upwards, and can be as high as 4 lbs.

In the big lakes, there is wet fly fishing in March, April, early May and September; dry fly fishing during the mayfly hatch—mid-May to early June—and in the summer evenings.

Some streams on limestone offer excellent dry fly fishing for big trout, particularly in late April, May and early June, and especially in the Robe (Co. Mayo), Black River (Galway–Mayo border), Maigue (Co. Limerick), Fergus (Co. Clare) and Little Brosna (Co. Tipperary). There is wet and dry fly fishing in many rivers and larger streams, and there are numerous small wet fly streams.

Fishing is free on many of the big lakes, also on many small lakes and rivers. The Inland Fisheries Trust, a state agency co-operating with angling clubs, controls many of the lakes and rivers, on most of which members may fish for

56

90 c. a year, with an extra charge of $4.80 a year for certain special fisheries. The other trout waters are controlled by angling associations whose angling subscriptions range from 60 c. to $4.80 a year. No rod licence is needed for brown trout fishing.

COARSE FISHING

The best coarse fishing—it is of very high quality in Irish waters—is in the upper and middle reaches of the Shannon, the upper reaches of the Erne, and the slow-flow rivers, canals and small lakes in Cavan, Clare, east Galway, Leitrim, Longford, east Mayo, Monaghan, Offaly, West-meath, Sligo, Roscommon and parts of Louth. The River Barrow (Co. Carlow) and the Munster Blackwater (Co. Cork) are also good waters. In most of these areas, coarse fishing is free.

Pike—average size 5 to 10 lbs.—are widely distributed. Twenty-pound fish are common, and 30 lbs. is the minimum weight accepted for claims by the Irish Specimen Fish Committee! Perch and rudd are also widely distributed, and the bream are plentiful. Roach and dace occur in considerable numbers, but only in the Munster Blackwater. Tench and carp are found in a few places, and are being introduced to others. No rod licence is necessary for coarse fishing.

SEA ANGLING

Some of the best sea angling in Europe is on the south and west coasts. In estuaries and from small boats there is excellent light spinning for big bass, and surf fishing on beaches which are not crowded. There is also rock fishing for pollack, wrasse and conger, and mullet abound in creeks and harbours. Tope are prolific in some areas, and can be caught on light tackle. In places like Achill, Ballycotton, Dungarvan and Kinsale, there is blue shark fishing, and big porbeagle and thresher are found on the west coast. Experienced boatmen and bait are available to visitors.

GOLFING

A survey by a leading American sports magazine revealed that Ireland has more golfing room per head of population than 18 of the 21 countries covered by the survey. In all there are over two hundred courses—including 20 first-class championship courses around the coast.

Although the courses are of high standard, the green fees are amazingly low. A first-class course and clubhouse can cost as little as 30 c. and will certainly not be more than 90 c. a day. In most cases, £1 ($2.40) to 25s. ($3) will cover a day's play, including the green fees, the caddy, your lunch and tea. The services of professionals are also very reasonable.

Because of the mild climate, courses are in playing condition all through the year, but the competition season is usually from March to October. Most of the clubs have an extensive "open" fixture list and visitors are particularly welcome. For golf spectators there are numerous Irish Championships and professional tournaments, including the Irish Hospitals' $12,000, 72-holes tournament in July.

Before visiting a club, it is advisable to contact the club secretary and obtain all the information you need about caddies, green fees, and catering facilities; also to find out whether there is a competition in the club on the day in question—although visitors are always welcome, a crowded course on such a day is not the best time to enjoy a friendly game.

Ladies can play every day of the week on all but a few of the Dublin courses, where Saturday play is restricted by the number of men's competitions. If you have not brought your own clubs, the local professional as well as members will be happy to lend you some. A list of golf clubs under their counties is available from Irish Tourist Offices.

SHOOTING

Shooting in Ireland for native game birds—pheasant, partridge, grouse and mallard—is under development all over the country, but is not yet available to any great extent. Shooting for migratory wildfowl, including duck, geese, snipe, plover and woodcock provides very good sport in many parts of the country.

SHOOTING RIGHTS

(1) Landowners: Shooting rights are privately held and are mostly in the possession of the landowners from whom prior permission for shooting must be obtained.

(2) Irish Land Commission: A large volume of shooting rights is owned by the Commission and can be rented for the season, or taken on lease for a period of years. Application should be made to The Secretary, Irish Land Commission, 24 Upper Merrion Street, Dublin 2.

(3) Department of Lands (Forestry Division): Details of shooting rights on State Forest Lands can be obtained from The Secretary of the Department, 22 Upper Merrion Street, Dublin 2.

FIREARMS

Shotguns, rifles and ammunition can be imported under licence, which is given free to any person who obtains a Firearms Certificate, both of which are issued by The Secretary, Department of Justice, Upper Merrion Street, Dublin 2. On the Certificate, applicants are required to give their name and address; type of weapon; and if possible the port of entry and address in Ireland. Fees, to be sent with the application, are, in the case of shotguns, $5.40 for the first and $1.20 for each additional gun. The fee for each rifle is $2.40.

GUNDOGS

So long as no contagious disease harmful to livestock or game currently exists in the home district, gundogs can be imported when accompanied by owners, and will not be subject to quarantine.

THE OPEN SHOOTING SEASON

The open shooting season for various kinds of game depends on the density of stock and preservation requirements. Details of the open season can be obtained from Irish Tourist Offices. In the 1963–64 season, killing or taking of Green Plover (Lapwing), Hen Pheasant, Barnacle Geese, Brent Geese, Greylag Geese, Quail and Landrail was prohibited throughout the country.

HOTELS

Some hotels are able to make shooting arrangements for their guests. This applies to those listed below (several of which are mentioned elsewhere in the book) but there is no guarantee that facilities will be given at any of these places at a particular time—application should be made to managements well in advance of an intended visit.

CO. CAVAN	Sheelin Shamrock Hotel, Mountnugent Park Hotel, Virginia
CO. CLARE	Old Ground Hotel, Ennis
CO. CORK	Munster Arms Hotel, Bandon
CO. DONEGAL	Malin Hotel, Malin
CO. GALWAY	Ballynahinch Castle Hotel, Ballinafad Glynn's Hotel, Gort Hayden's Hotel, Ballinasloe

CO. KERRY	Towers Hotel, Glenbeigh
	Butler Arms, Waterville
	Fitzgerald's Guest House, Annascaul
	Hotel Manhattan, Leebrook, Tralee
CO. LEITRIM	Bush Hotel, Carrick-on-Shannon
CO. MAYO	Old Head Hotel, Louisburgh
	Jeffers Railway Hotel, Westport
	Mount Falcon Guest House, Ballina
	Curraghmore Guest House, Ballinrobe
CO. OFFALY	Dooly's Hotel, Birr
	County Arms Hotel, Birr
CO. TIPPERARY	The Sail Inn, Dromineer, Nenagh
CO. WESTMEATH	Shamrock Lodge Hotel, Athlone
	Prince of Wales Hotel, Athlone

HUNTING

There are 85 recognised hunting packs in Ireland, some
of which were established in the eighteenth century, and
have preserved their original strain of hounds. Visitors
can hunt on most days of the week, and subscriptions for
the season range from $7 to $120, and cap-money from
30 c. to $4.80. A list of hunts is available from Irish Tourist
Offices. Horses can be hired at numerous centres, especially
in areas covered by hunts, and hunt secretaries will usually
advise enquirers of local stables from which mounts can be
hired, particularly during the hunting season. Hourly or
daily hire of horses and riding lessons are obtainable in and
around Dublin from eight different stables:

Lt.-Col. Hume-Dudgeon, Burton Hall, Stillorgan.

(Tel.: 893204)

Mr. T. H. Kellett, 39 Mespil Road, Dublin.

(Tel.: 61216)

Mr. W. Magee, 19 Montpelier Hill, Dublin.

(Tel.: 76021)

The Manager, Merrion Hall Riding Stable, Strand Road, Merrion (Tel.: 692883)

The Manager, Riding Stables, Old Connaught Ave., Bray.

Mrs. V. Cottell, Glencaraig Riding School, Old Bawn, Tallaght, Co. Dublin (Tel.: 592253)

Mr. S. Diffley, Westcroft Riding School, Beechpark, Castleknock, Co. Dublin (Tel.: 343278)

J. J. Magee, Main Street, Delgany, Co. Wicklow. (Tel.: Greystones 874449)

RIDING

In a country famed for its bloodstock, there are naturally many places at which horses and children's ponies can be hired from riding stables by the hour or the day. Pony-trekking is organised by the following hotels, to which application should be made for further details:

Bel-Air Hotel, Ashford, Co. Wicklow

Arnold's Hotel, Dunfanaghy, Co. Donegal

Towers Hotel, Glenbeigh, Co. Kerry

Lakeside Hotel, Killaloe, Co. Clare

Roxboro Hotel, Rostrevor, Co. Down

Arrangements for pony-trekking can also be made at other centres, some of which I have mentioned elsewhere in the book.

POLO

Dublin is probably the only city in the world where it is possible to watch polo entirely free of charge. The season lasts from May to August. The All-Ireland Polo Club, founded in 1874, is one of the oldest in existence, and has produced many of the leading players. Play takes place at the Polo Grounds, Phoenix Park, on Tuesday, Thursday and Saturday afternoons. In June and August, there are open tournaments for visiting teams. The subscription for playing members is $25. Pavilion membership is $2.50. Enquiries can be made from The Secretary, All-Ireland Polo Club, Phoenix Park, Dublin.

HORSE RACING

Horse racing is an important feature in Irish life. Not counting local point-to-point meetings, there are 150 fixtures in the Irish Racing Calendar, taking place on some 30 courses.

The Irish Sweeps Derby—the classic race for three-year-old colts and fillies at level weights over $1\frac{1}{2}$ miles—is run at the Curragh in County Kildare, where it began in 1866. The Curragh is 30 miles from Dublin, 130 from Cork, 106 from Shannon and 132 from Belfast. Adequate train services are operated to a station near the stands, and there are good views of the course from all parts of the enclosures. Other classic events held there are the St. Leger and the Guineas.

Steeplechasing takes place all through the year. The flat-racing season begins in March and ends in November, and point-to-point meetings are held during the spring months. Off-course betting is legal and there are turf accountants' offices in all towns. Some towns have special race weeks, combining horse racing with other sporting and social events. Killarney has one in mid-July; Galway Races are in the last week of July; Tramore Races are in mid-August and Listowel Races are at the end of September.

Bloodstock breeding is very big business in Ireland. Irish-bred racehorses worth nearly $8,000,000 were exported in 1961, during which year the produce of Irish stud farms, large and small won $3,650,000 in stake money in 22 different countries. There are about 100 thoroughbred stallions in Ireland, among them winners of English Classics and the Kentucky Derby.

FIELD SPORTS

Irish national games include Gaelic football (in which the players handle the ball but not each other!), hurling (a more strenuous kind of hockey) and handball. Football matches are well attended. So is the spectacular hurling. An unusual game of bowls is played with wooden balls on country roads. Iron bowls are used in Cork. Gaelic games are held at Croke Park in Dublin. The governing body for field sports is the Gaelic Athletic Association, North Frederick Street, Dublin.

WALKING AND CLIMBING

Outdoor enthusiasts need no telling that walking and climbing can be enjoyed in Ireland free of the restrictions about trespassing which may hinder them elsewhere. Because of this, the beautiful country can be appreciated to the full. Farmers are friendly and, if you are sleeping out on a walking or climbing holiday, usually allow you to camp on their land. You can also thumb lifts successfully, and with no need for embarrassment—the people accept this as normal.

Climbers will find more than 1,000 hills of heights ranging from 1,000 to 3,400 feet. The best are in the south and the west, but there are plenty to be tackled all over the country apart from certain stretches on the east coast.

You can obtain rock-climbing guides to Donegal and Wicklow from the Irish Mountaineering Club, 16 Lower

5. Aerial view, Rock of Cashel, Co. Tipperary

6. Ardmore Round Tower, Co. Waterford

7. Fr. Matthew Memorial Church and South Mall, Cork

8. Horse-drawn holiday caravans in County Cork

Mount Street, Dublin 2; and "An Oige"—the Irish Youth Hostels' Association—39 Mountjoy Square, Dublin, will give details of the hostels it operates in various parts of the country.

COMBINING BUSINESS WITH PLEASURE

The number of business men who like prospecting a little while on holiday increases every year, and Ireland offers them as big a welcome as ordinary tourists receive. Naturally there are less problems, too, in a country with a common language, and which is so short a distance away from England. Lack of this last advantage, incidentally, has not deterred numerous interests further afield, notably in the United States.

In April 1963 an OECD report praised the buoyant Irish economy, the result of an expansion programme which, between 1952 and 1963, increased by $89m. the exports of manufactured goods which had previously contributed little to the total. Many items in this category are made from imported raw materials. Compared with 1952, when they represented less than 6 per cent. of the total value of exports, they amounted to 22 per cent. of a very much enlarged total in 1963. The total value of exports for that year reached the record level of $470 million—a 12.3 per cent. increase over the previous year, and an 8.6 per cent. increase above the 1961 figure. Optimism was justified in 1964, when the total was expected to be $500-530 million. Britain, taking 60 per cent., is the biggest buyer of Irish goods. Export categories are listed under 46 groups in the Export Directory published by the Irish Export Board, a lively Government agency whose services include commodity information, introductions to suppliers, and co-operation in publicity and product promotion.

Industrialists interested in setting up manufacturing

subsidiaries in Ireland will find they can obtain valuable assistance from the Industrial Development Authority, a statutory organisation created by the Government. Its publications highlight the reasons why, apart from the many new Irish factories, more than 100 have been opened in the five years up to the beginning of 1964 by American, Belgian, British, Danish, Dutch, German, Swedish and Swiss concerns. Either independently or in association with Irish interests, they have established industries representing a total capital investment of $72 million and making a very wide range of products.

There are still many opportunities for development, especially for investment in new export industries, in a country well-placed geographically to serve the major European and North American markets. Advantages for investors also include: non-repayable cash grants which often amount to a substantial proportion of the total cost of factory site, buildings and machinery; tax-free export profits for ten years (there is no turnover tax, no sales, purchase or capital gains tax, nor any extra tax on distributed profits); a surplus of trainable labour, and the assistance of 300 technical schools (the country's four universities are also turning out an increasing number of scientists and engineers who would welcome new industrial posts at home). Many tributes have been paid to the willingness of Irish workers in co-operating with management and in learning new techniques, and wage levels compare favourably with those of other European countries. Foreign experts and technicians are welcomed because the need to import new skills is recognised.

Irish-manufactured goods usually enter Britain free of duty and benefit from preferential treatment in British Commonwealth countries. Capital and profits can be freely repatriated at any time. Further details of these and other advantages can be obtained from the Industrial Development Authority, 7 Mount Street Crescent, Dublin 2. Special facilities for raising capital are provided by another organisation set up by the Government, the Industrial Credit Company, Ltd., which underwrites capital issues and finances industrial undertakings by share investment and through medium and long-term loans. Its address is 26 Merrion Square, Dublin.

Many internationally-known companies are established on the industrial estate in the Customs Free Zone at Shannon Airport, which is of particular value to industries interested in air freight. Finished goods, partly-manufactured goods and raw materials whether dutiable or not (except narcotics, arms and other goods not normally admitted to the country) can be imported to the Free Trade Zone in any quantity. At Shannon, items can be manufactured, assembled, processed, packaged, graded, cleaned, marked, warehoused or handled in other ways, and there is no time limit for which goods may remain there.

Factory premises can be rented at Shannon, cash grants are offered, and export profits are totally exempt from tax until 1983. The area is particularly well supplied with labour, and housing is available for factory personnel. Shannon is an important stop for airlines operating on the transatlantic route, and many major companies have daily passenger and cargo schedules to European and North American capitals. Information can be obtained either from the Developments Manager, Shannon Free Airport Development Co. Ltd., at the airport, or the Industrial Development Authority at the above address.

NORTHERN IRELAND

Northern Ireland has also drawn industrial investors in recent years. Since 1945, when the Industries Development

67

Act became law, more than 170 British and American manufacturers, large and small, have located new plants in Ulster. As in Eire, they are notable for their broad range. Diversification, in fact, has resulted in the establishment of 135 new industries, mostly manufactures not made in Northern Ireland before 1945.

Through the Ministry of Commerce, the Government assists firms by giving grants, and letting factories at low rentals on long lease, in some cases with the option to purchase. Three types of factories are available. One is for the small business—the little man is very much encouraged. Another, of standard design, is built for the manufacturer, in a location he selects, and he pays the difference for anything he may require extra to specification. The third kind of factory, "the standard advance factory", is a type the Government has built in areas where unemployment dictated the need, and where all amenities and services are available. Even with these provisions the Ministry is very flexible in dealing with applications for new factories, all of which are treated on their own merits. When a project is obviously of special benefit to Northern Ireland, the Ministry will construct non-standard factories to a manufacturer's own specifications. The AEI Turbine Works at Larne is an example. There is also a scheme providing finance for those wishing to build their own factories or carry out modifications to existing premises.

Northern Ireland has a nucleus of skilled engineering workers and adequate trainable labour forces. Key workers imported to Northern Ireland can obtain housing. Executives, after living temporarily in hotels or rented houses, usually build or buy homes when they have been in the country for a year or more.

There are especially good transport services available to and from the country, including the well-known Transport

Ferry System, which provides door-to-door load delivery, dispenses with dockside handling and reduces the possibility of breakage. Internal road and rail services are also good.

Publications concerning industrial development facilities, including factory specifications, and on freight services to and from the country, can be obtained from the Ministry of Commerce, Chichester House, Chichester Street, Belfast 1, or the Northern Ireland Development Council, 13 Lower Regent Street, London, S.W.1.

THE INLAND WATERWAYS
OF
IRELAND
IN PARTICULAR
THE SHANNON
AND
BARROW NAVIGATIONS
THE GRAND CANAL
AND THEIR
SEVERAL LINKS WITH THE SEA.

PREPARED BY THE ATHLONE BRANCH OF THE
INLAND WATERWAYS ASSOCIATION OF IRELAND
H.J. & C. RICE. ATHLONE. 4TH APRIL. 1962.

PART TWO

BACKGROUND

HISTORY

Those of us who, through the years, have looked upon Ireland as a slow and backward country tend to forget that we English were still barbarians when—in the time of St. Patrick—she possessed one of the most advanced civilisations in Western Europe. This, and the fact that Ireland was never invaded by the Romans, underlines the pattern of her history.

While English history came to be founded very considerably on Roman settlements, the Irish people remained isolated instead of forming communities. When St. Patrick came, in A.D. 432, Christianity began to spread throughout the island and, as well as becoming the main centre of Latin learning, Ireland sent her Saints all over Western Europe, where they are commemorated in many places. Wealthy Irish monasteries drew the attention of the Norse sea-rovers who raided them from the parts of the coast they managed to occupy, having failed to conquer the country. Two centuries later, in 1014, they were defeated in battle at Clontarf.

The Irish provinces were ruled by kings who paid tribute to a "High King", who won power after battles between his and other families. In the twelfth century, Dermot MacMurrough, King of Leinster, rebelled against the High King then in power, and was banished. He appealed for assistance to Henry II of England, who gave him no direct support but allowed him to recruit fighting men in Britain.

Those who joined Dermot included Norman knights and mercenaries and the Anglo-Norman invasion of 1170 began a period of strife which lasted for centuries. It culminated with the defeat of the Irish cause at Kinsale in 1602.

However, only the eastern part of the country was affected by English institutions, the rest being occupied with clan-war and continued fighting with the English. Irish habits and customs even penetrated the "English Pale" around Dublin, and many English settlers later became Irish in outlook and sympathies. But the breach was enlarged when the Reformation left Ireland confirmed in the Catholic faith and England broke with the Pope to set up a national church.

During the sixteenth century, the Tudor kings began to extend English influence by settling in Ireland large numbers of English and Scots who dispossessed Irish tribesmen of their land and drove them to the west. The same thing happened under the first Stuarts, who gave a large area of north Ireland to Scottish settlers. Finally, while Charles I was fully occupied dealing with the mutiny of the Long Parliament, the Irish rebelled and killed thousands of the Protestant settlers in 1641. But Cromwell reconquered the country, took more land from the peasants and gave it to the English.

When James II was driven from England in 1689, Ireland supported him because of his efforts on behalf of Catholicism but, with an English army, and the aid of the Protestant north of Ireland, William of Orange—who had become William III of England—defeated James at the famous Battle of the Boyne in 1690. The "Orangemen", as the Protestants of Ulster became known, then held almost complete power in Ireland for a century and a half. Catholics could neither vote nor hold office. Catholic services were forbidden under penalty of death. All this legislation only had the effect of intensifying Catholicism in the country.

By the Act of Union with Britain in 1800, Ireland was persuaded to give up her separate Parliament, following which she had representatives in the British House of Lords and House of Commons. An attempt to secure repeal of the Act failed, but Catholic Emancipation was secured by Daniel O'Connell in 1829.

The terrible famine years of 1846–47, which began with a blight destroying the potato crop of 1845, were followed by mass emigration, reducing the population of eight million by half in the next seventy years. It was said, in the early 'thirties of the present century, that there were four times as many Irish in America as in the whole of Ireland. England had suspended and then repealed the "Corn Laws" which hindered the free import of grain but, apart from those who left the country, thousands died.

Risings in 1848 and 1867, and at other times, were suppressed, until some English statesmen began to undo old wrongs. Parnell, the Irish politician who detested violence, united other moderate elements and secured through Gladstone the passage in Parliament of a Land Act giving some stability to Irish agriculture, fixing fair rents establishing security of tenure. Another act allowed money to be freely spent in developing resources and lands, and to enable tenants to purchase their holdings. Gladstone also passed a law in 1869 disestablishing the English Church in Ireland, but he was unsuccessful in attempting to meet the constant call for Home Rule.

In 1898, the Conservative party gave Ireland a considerable degree of local self-government, and took many other measures to improve social and economic conditions, but the demand for Home Rule continued. The Liberals came to power in 1910 and in 1912 Asquith brought into Parlia-

75

ment the third Home Rule Bill, which became law just as the First World War broke out, because of which its operation was postponed. This led to the unsuccessful Easter Rebellion of 1916, for which 15 of its leaders were executed, thus further widening the breach between the two countries. Sir Roger Casement, who tried to bring German aid to Ireland, was hanged.

The leadership moved more and more into the hands of the Sinn Fein (it means "ourselves alone") the Irish revolutionary party, which openly endeavoured to make Ireland an independent republic. The party was not satisfied with the Home Rule Bill which Lloyd George had passed, establishing one Parliament for the six counties and another for the rest of the country. Although the situation was most acute, the "Ulster" Parliament was opened in 1921, and a conference took place in London between Irish republican delegates and members of the British Cabinet.

After nearly three months of negotiations, a treaty was signed, giving Ireland full dominion status in the British Empire, as the Irish Free State, with its own Parliament and Executive in Dublin. Many people still wanted an Irish Republic entirely independent of Britain and opposed the new state by force of arms, beginning the most awful of tragedies for any country—civil war. Ultimately, the Free State cleared up all resistance and those who opposed the Treaty eventually came to terms with constitutional authority.

Today, Ireland has the status of an independent republic, still anticipates a day when the whole country will be united. Northern Ireland, meanwhile, remains under the control of the British Parliament in which, unlike the Free State, it is still represented, although, for certain purposes, it has self-government.

TRACING YOUR ANCESTORS

Many years ago, in an American magazine, I saw a cartoon showing the office-door of a firm of solicitors. The name on the door was "O'Shea, O'Dea, O'Leary and O'Levy". Whether or not this splendid touch helped to break any race barriers, it was a great compliment to both nations.

On his Irish tour, the late President Kennedy found he had an enormous number of charming relations. He may not have been looking for them, but many visitors to Ireland do look for family links—and the Irish, in their disarming, only faintly commercial way, do everything possible to make ancestor-tracing not only easy, but also an excuse for a holiday in their lovely country! If you have Irish blood, this will give you added interest for your stay there. Those who may be holidaying at home for a change can still start the search by correspondence.

Either way, because Ireland's records have suffered from time to time in her turbulent history, not everyone will find all the material sought. The initial difficulty is that a particular Irish surname is borne by a considerable number of people, and this makes identification rather a problem. Accordingly, it is advisable to gather as much information as you can in your own country. Sources available to you include church and state records, family papers and the memories of older relatives. A local historical or genealogical society might be helpful, too.

What you need to find out at the beginning is the full name of your emigrant ancestor, his family background— whether rich or poor, merchants or farmers—his religion and the exact place from which he came. Many of the most important sources of genealogical information are located in Dublin. Records of births, marriages and deaths from the year 1864 are held at the Office of the Registrar-General in the Custom House. Marriages of non-Catholics are recorded from 1845. For a small fee you can obtain certified copies of entries, have a search made by officials or do it yourself.

Although the Four Courts building suffered very badly in 1922, the Public Record Office there contains a considerable amount of useful material, including the Tithe Appointment Books giving the names of those whose holdings were subject to tithes round about 1825; and the Valuation Records also relating to the first half of the last century. Here, too, are preserved wills and abstracts from wills and related documents. Another place where, for a small fee, you can make personal search, is the Registry of Deeds in Henrietta Street, which contains records from 1708.

A great many of the books in the National Library, Kildare Street, as well as old newspapers and manuscripts kept on file there, can yield very useful references. The Library has been preparing a huge card index which will facilitate searches here. It also has a Genealogical Office, housed in Dublin Castle, with its own collection of material, and where advice and information is given, without charge, about surnames, for instance. For a fee of $7.20 covering four hours' work, this office also carries out searches into its own or other records.

Church records remain the best source of information about the period before general civil registration. In urban areas, the parochial registers of the Catholic Church, in the custody of parish priests, often cover two hundred years or more, and those in rural districts usually begin about the second quarter of the last century. Many Church of Ireland parochial registers were destroyed at the Public Record Office in 1922, but some can still be found at parishes throughout the country, frequently dating back to the eighteenth century or even earlier. The Presbyterian Historical Society will try to help you if your ancestors were Presbyterians. Its address is Church House, Fisherwick Place, Belfast. In Dublin, there is the Religious Society of Friends, at 6 Eustace Street, who also may be able to help you.

If your ancestor or his forebears came from any of the northern counties, your search can begin in the Public Record Office of Northern Ireland, Law Courts Building, May Street, Belfast. The Tithe Appointments and other records for the six counties are held here.

Lastly, all over the country, tombstone inscriptions in cemeteries and elsewhere can often provide names and dates not available from any other source. Success cannot be guaranteed but as new information is constantly coming to light, your search may well be rewarded. In any event, it adds interest to your holiday.

FOLKLORE

In an out-of-print book about Ireland I read that no other country in Western Europe has so much folklore, and that its tales and legends have not been written but verbally passed on from each generation to the next.

They include stories of marriageable mermaids with removable tails, good and bad fairies. The bad fairies, it seems, run away with boys under twelve years old. Oddly enough, this does not give rise to much juvenile delinquency. Bad fairies can be thwarted, though, by dressing boys in red flannel petticoats so that they are mistaken for girls— knowing where that might lead the poor chaps, I imagine no-one does! (You noticed I said "imagine"?)

In a very Christian country, too, there are bigger and better ghosts than exist anywhere else. The banshee wails at night (but not, in my experience, for tourists) and phantom foxes prowl around Gormanstown (hunt, anyone?).

Peat fireside stories usually abound in the country districts, but I came across one town source of folklore talk. Leading you gently into the "commercial", Melina, the Irish perfume makers, explain the name of their "Shee-gwee" range as the Gaelic word for "the enchanted breeze" and consequently an apt description of the product. They go on to say:

"The Shee were the little people of Irish folklore; they were small and beautiful with a passionate love of music and dancing. The beauty of the Shee women, who were said to be more lovely than any mortal, has often been described in early Irish literature. An eleventh-century manuscript describes the fairy woman, Etáin, as follows:

'The hue of her hair seemed like
    the flower of iris in summer.
White as the snow of one night
    were her hands.
Dark as the back of a stag beetle
    the two eyebrows.
Blue as a hyacinth her eyes.
Her teeth like a shower of pearls.
Red as rowan berries her lips.
Soft womanly dignity in her voice.
The bright radiance of the moon
    was in her noble face.
The light of wooing in her regal eyes.
The walk of a queen had she.' "

Personally I think she was a crazy, mixed-up, technicolour fairy. Irish girls today are far more attractive than that, mingling some qualities of Etáin with many of their own, and in their case the *sound* of wooing—the lovely, rich, friendly "hallo" so many of them use in greeting—is liable to be quite misinterpreted.

Melina also talk of Midsummer's Eve which "has always been celebrated by the lighting of fires. In early times, it was thought that these fires banished sickness and scared off witches, who were said to be about on this night, the festival of magic. If the fire was to be effective, it was essential that the bone of an animal should be consumed in the flames, hence the bone fire. Any maiden who danced around nine bone fires before midnight would be wed within the twelve months. Flowers and herbs gathered on midsummer eve and woven into garlands would protect one from sickness and ill-fortune. Today the festival is celebrated as the anniversary of the birth of St. John the Baptist and is now more commonly known as St. John's Day.

"On the night of June 23rd, bone fires are still lit in the country, towns and villages of Ireland. The young sing and dance and play, and keep the blaze going, while the older people sit around the fire on chairs or upturned boxes, and re-tell stories of the Shee and of other midsummers."

The Cultural Relations Committee of Ireland publish a number of very interesting books in a series which includes *Saga and Myth in Ancient Ireland* and *The Ossianic Lore and Romantic Tales of Medieval Ireland*, both by Gerard Murphy. There is also a short amusing chapter on the subject in R. Lloyd Praeger's *Irish Landscape*, in the same series. Other publishers also have books on Irish folklore in their lists.

Anyone interested in folklore matters can write to The Irish Folklore Commission which is under the Honorary Directorship of the Professor of Irish Folklore in Dublin University, and has offices at 82 St. Stephen's Green, Dublin. The Commission is purely a research institution, and has no museum of exhibits. For this reason, visitors who wish to call there should first enquire in writing.

An Ulster Folk Museum was ready to be opened soon after my last visit, and I have indicated its location near Belfast in the Northern Ireland section of the book.

LITERATURE

In a guidebook, one cannot hope to deal adequately with the great wealth of Irish literature. For this reason, I have included below a summary of the subject, extracted from the most excellent *Facts About Ireland*, published by the Department of External Affairs, in Dublin, to whom I am very grateful for permission to reproduce the passage.

* * *

Manuscripts of the twelfth century contain the earliest surviving versions of the great Irish sagas and hero-tales and of the poetry written from the eighth century onwards by monks or by professional poets of the bardic schools.

In the Middle Irish period (1150–1550) the verse became more elaborate and stylised in form as the influence of the poetic schools became dominant. Poetry of the time can be divided into two types. Official or professional poetry was usually written in praise of a patron who maintained a poet or as a satire on one who had proved wanting in generosity. At the same time, there existed a more spontaneous poetry, mainly religious poems and love poems— *danta grá*. The latter particularly show the influence of other European literatures. Prose writings range from adaptations of classical or of French and English works (such as the Arthurian tales) to treatises on medicine, philosophy, history and genealogy.

Modern Irish writing begins in the seventeenth century.

The disappearance of the old Gaelic social order had ended the aristocratic patronage which the more formal bardic poetry had enjoyed and a different type of verse based on assonance rather than on stress, and associated with a popular rather than a court tradition, took its place. Through the following troubled centuries patriotic and religious poems and love songs in these new verse forms won a firm place in the hearts of the people.

English became the dominant language over most of the country in the course of the nineteenth century. The Irish language, however, did not die out and a movement for its re-establishment gained momentum at the end of the century. The leaders of the early phase of the revival were for the most part scholars or enthusiasts rather than great writers, but over the past two generations a number of younger poets, dramatists, short story writers and novelists have helped to provide the Irish language with a considerable modern literature.

The writings of Swift and Goldsmith in the early eighteenth century probably owe something to the exuberant tradition of Gaelic comedy, and the famous parliamentarian Edmund Burke is believed to have been a fluent Irish speaker. The poet Thomas Moore in the early nineteenth century was, however, the first Irishman writing in English to make a deliberate effort (in his Irish Melodies) to present something of the older Gaelic culture to the English literary world of his day. As English became more widely spoken in the nineteenth century many more Irishmen began to write in English—and the nationalist Young Ireland movement of the mid-nineteenth century and the research done on old Irish manuscripts in the 1840's bore fruit in a great literary revival at the end of the nineteenth century.

W. B. Yeats, winner of the Nobel Prize for Literature and the greatest of Irish poets who wrote in English, was the most prominent figure in this movement and drew on Irish mythology in his early poems and verse plays. John M. Synge, too, on the advice of Yeats, found his inspiration in Ireland—not in the ancient tales but in the traditions and dialect of the rural Ireland of his day.

The poets James Stephens, George Russell (Æ) and Pádraic Colum and novelist George Moore were other figures prominent in the Irish literary movement. But this movement was not confined to Anglo-Irish writing. It extended also to the Irish language, Irish culture and to Irish political separatism. These elements were fused in Pearse and other leaders who were later executed for their part in the 1916 Rising. They wrote essays, plays and verse in both Irish and English.

Meanwhile, Oscar Wilde and later George Bernard Shaw, also winner of the Nobel Prize for Literature, had been writing mainly abroad. James Joyce too left Dublin in the early 1900's to settle on the continent but he showed in all his work an intense and almost obsessive pre-occupation with the city and the decade he left behind. Samuel Beckett, one of a younger generation of Irish writers, has followed in part in Joyce's footsteps and now lives in Paris where he writes mainly in French.

At home, the short story has proved a favourite literary form with a new generation of writers and the work of Frank O'Connor, Seán O'Faoláin and Liam O'Flaherty is as well known abroad as in Ireland. Other novelists, dramatists and poets of a younger generation show much promise for the future.

PART THREE

TOURING IRELAND

DUBLIN

Not all Irish holidays begin in the capital, but it is the usual and most practical place at which to start. This is so even if you intend going immediately to the north or south; and because of its position as both entrance and exit, visitors can conveniently spend some time in Dublin before seeing the country, and more on their way home after a tour.

Cities are like symphonies. They have many moods and movements. There are times when they rise to a *crescendo*, others at which they are *tranquillo*. They are full of light and shade. And they have a beat, a tempo which also changes constantly. If I am ever at a loss to describe the way in which a city strikes me, I try to resolve the difficulty by making this comparison. Then I come up against the fact that one man writes a symphony, but many people contribute to the score of a city.

This is essentially true of capital cities, which are moulded by the glories and defeats, the ups and downs of their past history. Dublin's fair city is no exception.

One of the things which helps to prevent a travel-writer like me from becoming jaded is the anticipation with which I approach cities I am visiting for the first time. All of us—writers and readers—probably hold a mental picture of places that have had magic names from our childhood onward, and when we finally go to them we wonder whether they will live up to the image, be disappointing or more exciting than we expected.

Although Dublin was first recorded and praised by Ptolemy in A.D. 140, when it was called Eblana, and despite being aware of its long history, I must admit my first impression was of a fairly *new* symphony! But this was gleaned from what could be called the overtones—while walking down the immediate goal of O'Connell Street. This was just an initial feeling, one that disappeared at whichever of the many points I later turned off to explore. The width of the thoroughfare, as history shows, is by no means its only claim to fame, but internationally-reputed broad avenues I know in other countries lose much of their attraction when you look up at the commercial structures, big and small, which have gradually spoiled what was once a graceful building line.

Cities like Dublin have many exciting passages in their symphonies, and the trumpeters should use soft mutes when they reach the boring ones. O'Connell Street, as far as I am concerned, is strictly for shoppers rather than music-lovers. Having disposed of my main aversion at the outset—as I always do—I am ready for the solo spot in which to begin singing the city's praises.

Invariably, I like settling readers into their hotels before sending them on a sightseeing tour. Nowhere else in the world is this so fitting as it is in "Ireland of the Welcomes"— for Irish hotel-managers give true meaning to that description of their country. Without any harmful effect upon the relaxed efficiency to which I referred in my Introduction, they are ready to devote considerable time to new arrivals and assist them well beyond the scope of their normal work. They will help you plan your itinerary, tell you what to see and do and what to leave out; and within their own establishments, they will do their best to absolutely "kill" you with kindness. After a couple of days, you cease to be a newcomer, are treated virtually like a member of the family.

This can happen to you in a remote country hotel—or right here in Dublin.

My own hotel experiences in the city are indelibly engraved on my memory, for they began—if we may continue in musical metaphor—with a setting of the tone-poem by Mr. Eoin Dillon, General Manager of the *Shelbourne*. I became convinced very quickly not only that the "Little People" really do exist, but that Mr. Dillon is their uncrowned king. For all the time I was in his hotel, he kept pressing invisible buttons, causing desirable things to happen, in the hotel, elsewhere in the city, and at other places around the country which were on my route. Obviously, those unseen buttons were on the heads of myriad leprechauns. The response was certainly out of this world, clearly from theirs, and underlining their ability to make things go not—as popular belief has it—wrong, but delightfully right!

Perhaps none of this is surprising at the *Shelbourne*, when you realise that the Constitution of the State was written in one of the banqueting rooms on the first floor of the hotel in 1922. A copy can be seen in the room, which is preserved as it was at the time.

Apart from the hall porters, the first people you see on arrival at any hotel, before meeting the manager, are the reception staff. In many countries and countless hotels all over the world this can be a most off-putting moment. Those concerned are often remote, lofty, churlish, sometimes hardly stop short of being plain rude. As you would expect, prevalent though it is, this disease has not spread to Ireland, and the greeting of the girlies at the *Shelbourne* was sweet music. The same tune was played all through my stay— by the waiters, the porters and the upstairs maidens. And of course, the hotel chefs gave me and my family a foretaste of the excellent food, another of the things for which Ireland is highly reputed.

In the time between two visits I made to the hotel while writing the book, the once L-shaped restaurant was cleverly converted into two separate ones, so that the main room continues catering for the top-price diner, the now adjoining Saddle Room offers a midway budget, and the modern grill-bar opened a little while previously provides quick-meal service for even more moderate cost, from early in the morning until late at night. Mr. Dillon had a great deal to do with the design of the restaurant, and his architect has carefully carried out his ideas. The original cornice has been retained to blend happily with very tasteful contemporary decor and furnishings, specially created for the hotel and made in Dublin. Features are the unusual brass chandeliers and the drawings—not paintings—by Paul Hogarth, who illustrated the late Brendan Behan's *Ireland* and *New York*. The lighting, the soft mauve walls under the white cornice, and the two-tone yellow curtains at the big windows combine in a particularly pleasing effect at night. Incidentally, don't be put off by the apparent resistance of the big banquettes when you first sit on them—almost immediately afterwards, you find them very comfortable! I was impressed, too, by the slimline coffee cups, also designed by the architect.

The Saddle Room specialises in rib beef and steaks. Here you will not have to pay any extras, the price including vegetables, roll-and-butter and coffee. By the door is a Mexican-style saddle with solid silver mountings and spurs "loaned" by a wealthy American client of the hotel. The decoration is Canadian pine, and the upholstery is in rainbow tweed, a theme carried to the carpet; the main lighting has leather shades, made by a saddle-maker. Over the service counter—which has a studded leather front all too unfortunately obscured from general view—is a big copper canopy. In charge of the Saddle Room are Paul and

Christy, who take it in turns to look after you—and the service is very good, indeed.

Small dinner parties can be arranged in your own rooms. Drinking time can be spent either in the very comfortable lounge or the gay, recently-installed Horseshoe Bar. Three-quarters of the well-furnished rooms have private baths. From what my wife told me about the sumptuous powder room downstairs, many women would be content to stay there! In the foyer, incidentally, is a very useful shop selling papers, books, maps, cigarettes and other items. Overlooking St. Stephen's Green, the hotel—which belongs to the Irish group of the notable Trust Houses Ltd.—is peacefully yet conveniently situated for shops, theatres and sightseeing.

The other top hotel in the city is the *Gresham*. Situated on O'Connell Street—this is another convenient location, whether or not you share my feelings about that thorough-fare—the hotel is internationally-famed. So is its General Manager, Mr. O'Sullivan, who is reckoned, by all strata of society, to be "a character".

As well as the excellent cuisine, I was very much impressed with the accommodation, especially the splendid studio rooms—daytime sitting-rooms quickly transformed by efficient staff into bedrooms at night. They have private bathrooms, and heating which guests can control for themselves. The 50-foot terrace suites at the top of the building are the ultimate in luxury accommodation. These are furnished with hand-painted furniture, Irish carpets and linens and, in the sitting-rooms, Connemara marble fireplaces. Apart from studios and suites, most of the hotel bedrooms have private bathrooms. The unique Irish suites contain valuable paintings by Irish artists, and peat fires burn in their grates.

Celebrities from all walks of life stay at the *Gresham*.

For the same reason, the *Royal Hibernian Hotel* is also well-known. Its fame began when George IV visited the place two hundred years ago. Recently, architects, designers and interior decorators have been literally let loose inside the hotel. The resultant effect, while giving it an undoubted sparkle and great individuality, for my particular taste, is not exactly restful. This is peculiar to me, and I am sure that the place remains attractive to the majority of people.

The latest additions to the *Hibernian* include its luxurious penthouse floor; the Donegal Room, the Italian Garden Lounge with its water lily pool and fountain, and the *Lafayette* restaurant. The latter, designed by an American, commemorates the French general who fought with Washington in the War of Independence. A bust of Lafayette stands in one of its three rooms. Both generals are seen in one of two paintings hung there. The three rooms are separately called Maxim's; Joshua Dawson; and the Waterford, in which there is a fine chandelier of Waterford glass. Velvet-covered banquettes form part of the seating—I think these always help one's sense of well-being in any restaurant.

Also owned by the *Hibernian* management is the *Hotel Russell* on the other side of St. Stephen's Green. Here again you will find excellent food; a cocktail bar and comfortable lounges; some private suites and pleasant rooms most of which have private baths.

American visitors with experience of the Intercontinental group, which has hotels in many countries, will probably welcome the chance of trying the Dublin one, at Ballsbridge, ten minutes by bus from the centre, and only a block from the United States Embassy. It has a rooftop grill-room.

Two hotels I recommend, *Jury's* on College Green, and the *Moira* in nearby Trinity Street, are owned by what certain business circles like to call "a ball of fire". The very warm gentleman in question is Swiss-Irish Mr. Willy Oppermann, whose drive and enthusiasm for the work he has in hand are not only admired by his staff but others who come into contact with him as I did. At *Jury's*, there is a great deal of work in hand, to convert and expand the hotel into a very modern one which still preserves the Irish character. This is being achieved incidentally, on a wing by wing basis, in order not to upset the amenities of the hotel, which is remaining open all the time. The scheme should be complete by the time this is published. It includes transformation of the main dining-room into the *Portrait Restaurant*, which actually features portraits in the decor; and the addition of a large ballroom (just being rounded off during my last visit) in which, every night from the end of May to the beginning of September, "Siamsa Mor" takes place. This is an Irish entertainment presented as a cabaret with singers, dancers, harpists and humourists, at a cost of 10s. ($1.20). Food and drinks are also available, of course.

In *Jury's*, don't be surprised if the lift-boy knows which floor you want—each has a different colour-code which he can see from the tag on your room-key. Another touch planned and probably in operation by now is a system whereby if you ask for some room service and have not been answered by a certain time, an indicator light begins flashing in a control room, from where you are called and receive an apology for the delay. Of course, Mr. Opperman hopes you will not discover this refinement! In fact, it is a splendid piece of finesse, but all aspects of room service here are good. I particularly like the constant care of the private bathroom, and the evening check-up to see that everything is satisfactory. Hotels at home and elsewhere abroad could learn many lessons from *Jury's*. By the way, it is the first in Ireland to have air-conditioned bedrooms, which are also soundproofed. Other amenities include a rooftop garden and, apart from the main restaurant, a grill-room. Some private suites are available, as well as sitting-rooms which become bedrooms at night. Although the hotel has the most central position in Dublin, this does make it fairly difficult to park, another problem to be well resolved in due course, the management having bought an adjoining site on which it proposes to build a multi-storey car park. If you find any shortcomings, at *Jury's*, I shall be surprised. Apart from Mr. Oppermann, you may like to note you are in the good hands of Manager Robert Kerr.

You will be equally pleased with the associated *Moira Hotel*, which is more compact, but also has contemporary rooms with private baths and a number of private suites. Michael Collins is manager and here, too, improvement will have been made by the 1965 season, especially to the patio outside the Jardine Bar on the ground floor, where, amid exotic tropical plants, you will be able to dance to a trio. The hotel has a restaurant, a food-bar, and the "Executive Grill".

A small hotel worth mentioning is the *Ivanhoe* in Harcourt Street, and at the other end of the scale an expected addition to the city's hotels, the *Dublin-Hilton*, at the time of my last visit, was about to be erected on a site near the centre and not far from the airport.

I agree with the many who class Dublin as one of the most attractive capitals in Europe. Certainly it is a friendly place, and although it is the only city in Eire big enough to bustle as English and Continental cities do, the bustle seems to be confined to one area. In fact, reverting for a moment to our symphony, its main movement is a whirlpool that centres on College Green, O'Connell Street and its bridge, extends to Parnell Square and Grafton Street. Somehow, beyond these points, it seems to soften, as for instance, in Merrion Square where the traffic flow eases and there are rich brick tones in the Georgian houses all around; in nearby St. Stephen's Green, a point at which to stop for a few bars' rest. Another quiet passage inserts itself even while you stand on O'Connell Bridge, from which you may look down to see a misty radiance on the waters of the River Liffey. I was not the first to notice this "claret glow" as Seán O'Faoláin called it—such beauty cannot escape the beholder especially if he is a recorder, too.

The musical distillation of which Dublin is composed has its odd notes, too, for example in the Nelson Pillar, bearing a statue of the great admiral. If you pay the small fee which allows you to climb the spiral staircase inside the column, you will not learn why a man who had nothing to do with Ireland should be so honoured. One writer has said the reason is simply that Nelson was a hero, and the Irish love heroes. A high point worth looking for, by the way, is the graceful spire of the Abbey Presbyterian Church in nearby Parnell Square. There you will also find the Gallery of Modern Art.

Whatever else you miss, it is not easy to overlook the big Bank of Ireland on College Green, one of the finest buildings in the city. You are also expected to be impressed by the Customs House—some even describe it as one of the noblest buildings in Europe—but much as I love Ireland, I am bound to say this does not excite me. It may do something for you, but I go to Italy for architecture, to Ireland for natural rather than man-made beauty. My Irish friends will take this more kindly when I say that exceptions are found in many churches—especially ruined ones!— and certainly in Dublin's Protestant Cathedrals, St. Patrick's and Christ Church. In fact, I will make amends more fully by saying that St. Patrick's is one of the finest I have seen anywhere.

Below the architraves are five windows, two at either side falling away from the central one where a greenish light comes through. Then there is a row of three lovely, delicate double porticos and, below this again, recessed behind the wonderful arch over the altar, are three very beautiful windows, giving the effect of an illuminated Persian carpet. Over what used to be the Knights' Stall are their helmets, swords and coats of arms. Also interesting is the gold mosaic panel and cross, part of the memorial to the men of the fifth, seventh and eighth battalions of the Royal Irish Regiment who fell in the South African war—above this, too, is another fine window. The interesting histories of both St. Patrick's and Christ Church—the latter has a pleasant garden forecourt—are contained in well-written booklets they have on sale, and both buildings repay exploration. St. Patrick's contains the tomb of Jonathan Swift, who was Dean from 1713 to 1745, and his beloved Stella is buried nearby.

While you are near Christ Church, you will see a turning where High Street becomes Cornmarket. From a flight of steps alongside St. Audoen's, the oldest parish church in the city—founded in 650—you can walk down to St. Audoen's Arch, the only gate and all that is left of the wall of the town as it was in Norman times. Two large towers and part of the curtain are also all that still stands from this period in Dublin Castle which is built on the site of an early Danish fortress, and dates from the beginning of the thirteenth century. The Castle was the official residence of English viceroys when Ireland was under British rule. Reconstruction work has been in hand here recently, but this has probably been completed by now, in which case the State Apartments may be open to visitors. The Heraldic

9. Kinsale,
   Co. Cork

10. The Blarney
    Stone,
    Castle Blarney,
    Co. Cork

11. Golf at Killarney

12. The Spanish Arch, Galway

Museum and the Church of the Most Holy Trinity are open on weekdays and Saturdays, and the Castle Yard is always open.

The famous Book of Kells, an illuminated manuscript dating from the eighth century, is among the possessions of the Trinity College Library, which is open to the public all through the year. Two other buildings to see are the Four Courts, on the quays, and the Queen Anne Mansion House, official residence of the Lord Mayor, in Dawson Street. The city guide gives full details of these and any other buildings you may want to take in—I have mentioned only those that are outstanding.

The museums and galleries, of course, contain a great deal to interest visitors. In the National Gallery, on Merrion Square, there are several Titians, and Michelangelo, Tintoretto, El Greco and Goya are among the other masters represented. I particularly noted Mazzolino di Ferrara's "Pharaoh and his host overwhelmed in the Red Sea", and of the collection of Irish works found those of Jack Yeats very unusually individual and exciting. The National Museum, in Kildare Street, contains antiquities, fine arts other than painting, geology and other sections. Important exhibits include the eighth century Ardagh Chalice and Tara Brooch; the twelfth-century Cross of Cong, Lismore Crozier and Shrine of St. Patrick's Bell. Also striking is a 52-feet dugout canoe, one of the largest specimens found in Western Europe—this one came from County Galway. The Museum and the Gallery are open on weekdays and Sunday afternoons.

I have already referred to the Municipal Gallery of Modern Art in Parnell Square. This is closed on Mondays, open on other weekdays and on Sunday mornings. Another museum which must be mentioned is the Joyce Museum at Sandycove, which was opened in 1962 by the late publisher of the author's *Ulysses*. Housed appropriately in the Martello Tower which he featured in this famous work, and where he lived for a time, the collection is of first editions, some letters, photographs and personal items, as well as the death mask. It is open in the afternoon from June to September.

Long established in the city but using modern methods, is a building known as the biggest brewery in the world where, if you are not quite sure whether the well-known stout is good for you, you can receive a glass at the end of a conducted tour.

Top in size is also the claim for Phoenix Park, at 1,760 acres the largest enclosed public park in the world. Part of it is given over to the 132-year-old Dublin Zoo, other areas to the President's house, the American Embassy residency, the Papal Nunciature, and the famous Racecourse. You would have to state your business in some of these places, but the first and last, of course, are very much open to visitors, as are the large areas in which you can roam as freely as the herd of deer you will see there. A fine collection of wild creatures in the zoo includes bears, chimpanzees, camels, elephants, giraffes, hippopotami, lions, monkeys and rhinos. These and the many exotic tropical birds are housed in modern buildings or enclosures without bars. In the children's Pet's Corner are ducks, guinea pigs, kid goats, lambs and other animals gentle enough for them to handle. Lion cubs are sometimes among them—Dublin Zoo, famous for its lions, sends cubs all over the world. Apparently this success is the result of feeding the lions on donkey and goat meat, similar to the diet they would choose in their native surroundings.

There is a large lake, well laid-out gardens, a restaurant and shops. The zoo is open from 9.30 a.m. until 6 p.m. in summer or sunset in winter, on weekdays, and from midday on Sundays. Lions and tigers are fed at 4 p.m. in summer, 3 p.m. in winter; penguins and pelicans at 4.15 p.m.; sea-lions at 4.30 p.m. in summer, 4 p.m. in winter.

Two of Dublin's theatres, the *Abbey* and the *Gate*, are well-known internationally. The *Abbey*, founded in 1904 by Yeats, Lady Gregory and the Fay brothers, was burned down in 1951 and while a splendid new building is under construction, its high standards of production and performance are continued at the *Queen's Theatre* in Pearse Street. Irish companies usually play modern drama and revive the classics at the *Gate* in Parnell Square. The little *Pike Theatre*, first to produce plays by the late Brendan Behan, now specialises in fast, witty revues. Programmes at the *Gaiety* in South King Street range from grand opera through musical comedy, drama and ballet. West End successes, Irish dramas and musicals are played at the *Olympia*, in Dame Street.

Of the considerable number of annual events in the city, the most important and well-known are the agricultural Spring Show in May, the Dublin Horse Show in August— both held at Ballsbridge; and the International Theatre Festival in September.

To know cities, you have to stay in them longer than most people can or want to spare on a holiday, but if your visit here is an extended one, you cannot do better than consult the excellent *Green Guide* to Dublin, on sale in many places, and which gives you far more detail than I have room for—because my job is to take you round the whole country! You can also obtain information while in Dublin from the bureau of the Irish Tourist Association, 15 Upper O'Connell Street, which is open from 9 a.m. to 7.30 p.m., or from the Tourist Information Centre in Creation Arcade, Grafton Street, open from 9.30 a.m. to 5.30 p.m.

A few things I hope you won't miss as you wander round

the city are the Metal Bridge on the quays, once called "Halfpenny Bridge" when that was the amount of a toll there, and the shop of the Dublin Woollen Company facing one end—this has been on the site since 1888 and has a marvellous collection of tweeds for sale; the gay blue and white rococo façade of Sheeran's Auction Rooms on Bachelor's Walk, where, as in the city's many antique shops, you will find some worthwhile pieces; the typical coffee houses which are a feature of Dublin, especially around Grafton Street, and in contrast, the *Paycock*, a very modern one in Dawson Street; and the *Country Shop* on St. Stephen's Green, near the *Shelbourne*—it sells basketry, wrought iron, pottery and tweed, and serves melty cakes, a good cup of tea, the wonderful Irish soda bread (I usually bring a dozen loaves home with me!) and inexpensive lunches. This is part of an organisation doing its best to foster handicrafts.

In case sightseeing wears out your shoe-leather, there are while-you-wait repair shops on the Grafton Street corner of St. Stephen's Green, and in Cavendish Row by Parnell Square. Finally, if you consider it important to be earnest about such things, you can stare at the house in Merrion Square where Oscar Wilde was born. When you have done the rounds, you can return to *Davy Byrne's* in Duke Street—the "moral pub" of James Joyce's *Ulysses* or, to end on the musical note with which we started the tour of the capital, at a "singing pub"—first making sure it is one of that kind, as the others do not welcome the sound.

A sound linked with something that has been brought back from the past is that of horses' hooves. Several of the cabs which used to be a feature of Dublin streets during the last century have been repaired and painted. Together with some old family broughams which have been donated for the purpose, they can be hired for sightseeing—so that even in one of the few bustling places of Ireland you can slow down the pace if you wish!

Within easy reach of the city are Blackrock seaside resort (4 miles); Dun Laoghaire, where the cross-Channel steamers come in and there are various amenities (7 miles). Dalkey, 2 miles further on, claims to have a continental flavour. On the slopes of its hill is Torca Cottage, where George Bernard Shaw lived between 1866 and 1874. Two miles beyond Dalkey is Killiney, which has a fine beach. So have Portmarnock, 7 miles from the city, Malahide, 9 miles out, and Skerries, 18 miles distant. The bureaux mentioned above, and the C.I.E. offices will give you details of the various tours which can be made while keeping Dublin as a base, and the following sections of the book are for those who want to move on with me and see the beautiful country.

DUBLIN TO WEXFORD AND WATERFORD

Long periods in a travel-writer's life are spent away from home, so for their sake and mine, I try to take my family away with me on two trips a year. They came on my first visit to Ireland, because my wife had hankered to see the country for some time. After our wonderful welcome in Dublin, we drove off to begin a tour of the most interesting places in the south, and only a few miles had slipped by before we wondered why we had not come here much sooner —to enjoy the peacefulness we like and which is found in very few places today.

We came to the delightful village of Enniskerry, lying 12 miles from the capital, in a wooded hollow surrounded by the hills west of Bray. Nearby is what instantly became one of my favourite spots, the lovely Powerscourt waterfall, in the Deer Park of Viscount Powerscourt's fine mansion house. As elsewhere, the deer herds are exciting, but it was the waterfall that took my breath away. There are mightier and more magnificent falls in other countries, but this one had an effect upon me which is difficult to describe. I was not overawed, but mellowed. I felt very peaceful and content as I watched the cascade tumbling down its 400-feet cliff, the ridge of a hill to its left, and the sheep grazing below, in the wide spaces between occasional tall trees. My family went along the curved path to examine the fall at close quarters, but I was certain the magic would go if I joined them, so I stayed by the car, and took pictures which, good as they may be, couldn't quite capture the moment, although they record the softness of the setting.

Powerscourt House rises up on high ground above its lawns, and in its gardens—open to visitors daily—there are ornamental pools with water lilies, statues and, in season, many rhododendrons. The Venetian Gate was made by Moise della Toure in Venice. Other items of interest are the statue near the Green Pond, of a Maltese poodle dog, pet of the sixth Viscountess Powerscourt; the cemetery on one of the slopes where all the family's pet dogs and ponies lie buried; the tree—one of the "monkey puzzle" type—which came from South America and is thought to be the only one of its kind in Europe; and the Japanese Garden.

There is also a tower, the design of which was based on a three-inch silver pepper pot. Around this are cannon from the Spanish Armada, the Battle of the Boyne, the Franco-German War, and H.M.S. *Repulse*; also a water clock and an ancient granite corn-grinding mortar, the latter discovered underground as recently as 1945. The wall behind the tower encloses the family burial ground. The terraces were designed by a Mr. Daniel Robertson, who was wheeled about the place in a wheelbarrow, grasping a bottle of sherry. His daily designing ended when the bottle was empty and his peculiarities did not prevent one hundred men with horses and carts from carrying out a splendid piece of landscape gardening.

A café and souvenir shop are located near the entrance to the gardens, where cut flowers, pot plants and eggs are on sale. Have a look for the fine St. Bernard dogs in their pen near the entrance. The demesne also houses the Ferguson School of Mechanised Farming.

Outside the village there are signs to the house and the waterfall, and if, as we did, you go first to the fall, you will find a lodge where you can buy tickets also giving admission to the grounds, which stretch for five miles. Coming out of the same lodge gate after seeing the fall, turn left and drive into the grounds through the first gate on the right. The Deer Park closes at 8 p.m.

We cut across to Bray, a small seaside resort with a good, safe beach but spoiled as these places often are in most tourist countries, by a clutter of ice-cream parlours and amusement arcades—but notable for the *Royal Hotel*— and then went on to Greystones, once a fishing village and now a quiet resort and residential area. Here, too, there is a good sandy beach, a golf course, a riding school with horses for hire nearby, and the homely *La Touche Hotel*. I had heard a lot about this place, and although it seemed rather deserted when we arrived, its popularity and one of the reasons for this were apparent when we went into the dining-room for lunch. We were first there, sat at a table near to and facing the windows. One or two residents came to their tables within our vision, and I was aware of growing chatter behind me. Before finishing the soup, I looked round and saw the room was full of people who not only treated meals as absorbing breaks in their days, but knew they would enjoy good food on each occasion.

Like most of the hotel managers I met—and it's liable to happen to you, too—Mr. and Mrs. Fitzgerald of *La Touche* asked me to pass on goodwill messages to their opposite number at my next port of call in Glendalough. We drove there on a road the side of which was covered in yellow and purple heathers, through moors cloaked in many different greens. We chose this route instead of the road near the coast to Wicklow, and it goes through Sally Gap, Lough Dan, and the pretty villages of Roundwood and Annamoe.

In a valley of untamed beauty lies Glendalough, which has considerable scenic and historical interest. "Our man" in Glendalough was Mr. Casey, Manager of the *Royal Hotel*. Gentle but full of the enthusiasm typical of his calling in this country, he is my idea of what the "little people" are really like—when, while living mostly in their world, they also have to cope with existence in ours. Again in the manner of his calling, he stopped work to take us on a tour of the highlights which, in Glendalough, are the two lakes and the ruins of the monastic settlement founded by St. Kevin.

I will mention the places we saw with Mr. Casey, and strongly recommend you to ask him, if you want detailed accounts, for the informative booklet guide *Glendalough and the Seven Churches of St. Kevin*, by P. J. Noonan, a citizen of Wicklow.

Some of the ruined buildings date from A.D. 618, the year that St. Kevin died; and the impressive 110-feet Round Tower, over a thousand years old, is in almost perfect preservation. So is St. Kevin's Cross. The church named after him is one of the most interesting of the ruins. In the face of the cliff some 30 feet above the far side of the upper lake is St. Kevin's "Bed", where the saint retired to pray. This, as Mr. Noonan points out, was originally a prehistoric tomb cut from the rock, similar to many found in countries the coasts of which faced the Mediterranean. A boatman will ferry you across the lake.

The *Royal Hotel* is well-known to British visitors, as a cosy and friendly old building, which has recently been modernised. It makes a good base for a few days' stay, especially if, with time to spare for lingering, you take Mr. Casey's advice and plan the first of four days in Glendalough; the second seeing the Wicklow Gap, Blessington Lakes and Sally Gap (now you know in advance, you can take in Sally *en route* from Dublin!); the third in Glenmalure, Aghavannagh and Auchrim; and the last on the Ballard Road across the mountains to Glenealy.

At the summer shop of the Avoca Handweavers, opposite the *Royal Hotel*, persuasive Mr. Esmonde talked me into buying my wife a striking woollen hat called a "thatcher". Back home, many women who see it in its bright orange glory go (Emerald Isle) green with envy. Now I understand even more why hats are among the things that do most for female morale. The parent shop is on the north side of Avoca, for which we next headed, cutting out Wicklow.

The county town is only 5 miles beyond Glenealy, and could easily be taken in on the day excursion suggested above which includes that attractive village. Wicklow, although considerably modernised, still preserves some of its early character in the narrow streets which remain, and is a resort with a very long beach. To the south is Silver Strand, another good beach. There is safe bathing from both and amenities include boating, golf, fishing—for small brown trout in certain streams. Brittas Bay, also on the south side, has a fine sandy beach.

Like Glendalough, Avoca is a good base from which to visit Glenmalure, Lough Dan and Lough Tay. Three miles north of Avoca is the Meeting of the Waters, a notable beauty spot where the Avonmore and Avonbeg rivers join.

Above is Castle Howard, and nearby is the bare skeleton of poet Tom Moore's Tree.

More sandy beaches make Arklow a favoured holiday resort, where there are bathing, boating, golf and tennis facilities; and those small brown trout pop up again in the Rivers Ahare, Aughrim and Ennereilly. Sea fishermen will find bass between Arklow and Wicklow Heads. The *Arklow Bay Hotel* is a very good one.

Near Woodenbridge, west of Arklow, is the Croaghan Kinsella mountain, source from which the goldsmiths of ancient Ireland obtained much of their material. In prehistoric times, Irish gold-workers in this district dominated the trade, a point underlined by scientists in a 1963 report of their tests on the Moulsford torque, a gold necklace unearthed in Berkshire three years before, and made in 1200 B.C. A nugget found at Croaghan Kinsella in 1796 led to a gold rush, the finding of 2,600 ounces in a few months, and a much larger amount in later periods.

A modern shrine at Arklow Rock encloses a well with water said to have curative properties and which up to recent times pilgrims visited annually on 25th March. An old custom still seen was the practice of tying a little piece of cloth to the hawthorn tree when taking the water. Another interesting item at Arklow Rock is "The Hanging Stone", very big and so finely balanced on the one below that it seems only a touch would send it crashing down.

After leaving Arklow for Gorey, there is a good wide, well-surfaced road which continues for some distance although it narrows later. A turning off this road leads to Titania's Palace, which is well-signposted and very much worth a diversion.

It is a sixteen-room model palace of a fairy queen, designed and created by Sir Neville Wilkinson, an author and artist of the 1920's. Opened by the late Queen Mary, it was exhibited at Olympia, and has toured the world, earning money for crippled and neglected children. Not only were many of its parts and furnishings contributed by other distinguished people of the period, but there are items from Sir Neville's collection of what, in his guide to the palace (obtainable there) he calls "tiny-craft". In one room, for instance, is a cannon made by the Nuremberg armourer, Michael Mann, about 1580. The detail of this wonderful miniature conception is fantastic, and understandably delights children and adults alike.

Leaving Gorey, on the way to Enniscorthy, watch for the rockery and shrine on a bridge before you reach the village of Camolin. The grey-and-white striped front of the *Portsmouth Arms Hotel* on the bridge over the river is only one of the colourful buildings which line the banks on which Enniscorthy stands; and the squared Norman castle, rebuilt about 1586, is perfectly preserved, having been damaged considerably by Cromwell's guns in 1649. It was used as a prison during the Insurrection of 1798, restored for use as a residence in the nineteenth century.

As you come into Wexford, the Irish name of which is Loch Garman, you cross a bridge over part of the lake, before which is a ruin with one of those pencil-shaped lookout towers you often see around the country. Wexford is not an exciting place, and you would do well to plan it just as an overnight stop. This will enable you to stay at the *Talbot Arms*, a splendid experience in no way indicated by its unimaginative reception hall. The rooms and bathrooms are up to date and well appointed. So is the pleasant cocktail bar. There is an old-world tavern and a useful crafts shop in the foyer, where I could always find my wife when she was missing. The great revelation here is the restaurant, which has been justly praised by all the leading international guides to Europe, and in which most excellent food comes

107

to your table with the kind of service one usually expects to find only at places in big cities. It's nice to know that Manager Patrick Fitzpatrick shares my belief that anybody can do anything so long as the desire exists.

In fact, he is so confident of his ability to satisfy you that he has included on the hotel leaflet the names of all his key staff members to whom you are welcome to complain if necessary—a touch I liked very much. After the kind of dinner you will have here, at least a short walk is essential. Take the opportunity of doing the little sightseeing that can be done—the ruins of the twelfth-century Selskar Abbey, near the Westgate tower; the site (that's all you can see) of the Bull Ring in the town centre; and the Franciscan Church in John Street, which has large *lacunari* (square-recessed) stucco ceilings, coloured windows not visible from the street, and contains, under the Altar of St. Francis, the remains of St. Adjutor, a boy martyr of ancient Rome. Oscar Wilde's mother was born in a house on North Main Street, where there is also the birthplace of Sir Robert McClure, discoverer of the North-West Passage. American visitors will be interested in the memorial on Crescent Quay to "Gallant John Barry"—Commodore Barry, "Father of the American Navy". *White's*, in what was the old rectory, is another good comfortable hotel.

The town is historically important as the place where the first Anglo-Irish Treaty was signed in 1169, and where Henry II did penance, in 1172, for the murder of Thomas à Becket. An important annual event is the Wexford Opera Festival.

South-west of the town, facing Bannow Bay, is a house partly built from the remains of Tintern Abbey, named after the one on our River Wye, monks from which occupied it after its foundation about 1200 by William le Mareschal, Earl of Pembroke. Masonry from the abbey was also used in building the present church and a nearby bridge.

108

The normal route from Wexford to Waterford—avoiding a drive through the waters of Waterford Harbour!—is via New Ross, a pleasant little town where I stopped to look at the Church of St. Mary and St. Michael, which has an unusual façade and is set in a high position. Around the fine altar, there are frescoes on the walls and above, a painted, timbered section of roofing. Alongside the altar is a little blue-decorated Lady Chapel. The uncommon pulpit is a mosaic of marble and gold, and there is a chiming clock in the centre nave.

Waterford has many similarities to Wexford. Historically important and coastally-situated, it boasts a particularly outstanding hotel. Additionally, of course, it is famed all over the world for its glass, made in the factory at Johnstown—to tour which you must book in advance, preferably a few days ahead. This is unfortunate unless you make arrangements from home before departure, or on arrival in Ireland knowing that you will be covering much ground prior to reaching Waterford, because it is not a town in which you are likely to spend much time, despite the temptations of the *Tower Hotel*. Small parties of six are taken round the factory every half-hour, and the tour takes half-an-hour. Children are not allowed in—I can appreciate the reasons for this but again, I think it is a pity.

The huge circular building at the end of the quay is called Reginald's Tower (from which the hotel takes its name) and dates from 1003. Originally a Danish fortification, it has since been a Norman fortress, a royal residence, a mint, an armoury, a barracks and a city prison. It is now a museum, housing exhibits which include the many Royal Charters the city has received.

Newly-built in 1962, the *Tower Hotel* is an example of the best in contemporary design and furnishing. Rich Irish carpets and colourful tweed curtains strike bright notes in

109

the spacious public rooms and comfortable bedrooms—
the latter all have private baths or showers. There are
several two-room suites, and family suites which contain
bunk beds for children, with bulkhead lights, special ladders
and their own radios; a cocktail lounge and two other
lounges; a charcoal grill. The restaurant and the grill offer
French cuisine applied to good Irish food. The *Grand
Hotel* at Tramore—a seaside resort 8 miles from Waterford
where there is a long, sandy beach—is under the same
management as the *Tower*. A voucher transfer service is
operated between the two hotels, enabling guests to charge
to their account at the *Tower* services of both bar and
restaurant at the *Grand*. Both Tramore and Waterford
have eighteen-hole golf courses.

A brochure sponsored by the Waterford Junior Chamber
of Commerce contains a list of places at which you can stay
with an Irish family in the area. Members of amateur
musical societies in Britain will know that, apart from glass,
Waterford is noted for its annual Festival of Light Opera,
the only competitive one in the world. It is held in the
Theatre Royal which, unlike so many others in recent years,
was saved from closure and conversion to offices by local
theatre-lovers. As well as the old and familiar productions
in the light opera field, presentations have included the more
recent *Salad Days*, and among other events taking place
at Festival time, there have been a donkey derby and waiters'
races on Tramore Racecourse; sea angling and a midnight
barbecue at Dunmore East; and a Carnival Dance in
Waterford. During the Festival period (September) too,
shopkeepers offer very reasonable prices to visitors.

WATERFORD TO CORK

Reserve some time, before going on to Cork, to see at
least a part of the lovely Comeragh Mountains area.

If you can actually extend your stay at Waterford, you can drive to Ballymacarbry and contact Paddy Melody at *Melody's* pub there—he will set you up for pony-trekking in an area which is slowly coming to tourists' attention. Paddy's telephone number is Ballymacarbry 6.

Those with less time to spare can make a diversion to see some of the area from the main Cork road—a good one. Ten miles east of Dungarvan, the rich, dark-toned mountains can be seen as a background to the patchwork of fields, farms and trees. At Lemybrien, turn right for Kilrossanty. From there, take the first major turn to Kilbrien. After Kilrossanty, you will see a stone cross on top of a green hill to your right. Fuchsia bushes grow in profusion all around the district. There are rich purple carpets of heather with yellow and dark green patches between, on which creamy sheep are grazing. Here, beyond Kilbrien, look back at the distant sea from the lay-by you will reach. In the immediate foreground, there are conjoining slopes, one a patch of purple, the other a triangle of greens. Beyond a dark, humpy hillock, and between this and the sea, is another patchwork of green and golden fields (in September) —even when heavy cloud hangs nearby, the sun lights these colours magnificently.

In case you can manage the longer run, your route over the mountains would be via Kilmacthomas, Rathgormick, and, from the junction with Clonmel road, on to Ballymacarbry. Then return on the main Clonmel-Dungarvan road in the Dungarvan direction for about four miles, to Beary's Cross. There turn left and make for Kilbrien via Scart Bridge. Bear left at Kilbrien. You are then on the Mauma road from which you can find your way to the Cork road. That is a run of about two hours, all on tarred road, except for a quarter of a mile. On the short run, at Kilbrien, turn right to Scart Bridge and then go on to Dungarvan.

Along this road, the scenery changes. You will find yourself driving past tall firs, and on a hill a little way out of Dungarvan on the Youghal-Cork road, there is a lay-by with a glorious view of several bays around the town, of the coastline and open sea beyond. Beware of pied wagtails which, seemingly bearing lives as charmed as any cat's, are liable to cross quite calmly in front of the car. The run to Youghal, with sea views, is very smooth. Before the town, there is a graceful bridge, rather like Waterloo Bridge, and soon we were passing under the Clock Gate. Youghal—you pronounce it Yawl and it means Yew Wood—once a fortified city, is now a resort with a five-mile beach, and all the usual boating, fishing and golfing facilities.

Sir Walter Raleigh was once mayor of the town. In the garden of his Elizabethan house, Myrtle Grove (unfortunately closed to visitors) he planted the first potatoes grown in Ireland and smoked the first tobacco. Youghal is well-known for its boldly-patterned point lace, but its most remarkable characteristic is its high summer temperature (65 degrees) and exceptional record of sunshine, which enables figs, nectarines and other sub-tropical plants to grow there.

En route for Cork is the attractive little town of Middleton, which has a wide main street where we spotted a promising-looking gift shop. Here and elsewhere in the area, there are limestone caves with interesting dripstone formations.

Cork is a well-laid out, spacious and gracious city with much to engage the interest of visitors, but what struck me most about the place was the number of churches seen on its skyline at all levels. It is the second largest city in Ireland and although many cultural institutions have grown from its origins as a centre of learning at the end of the sixth

112

century, it is also a very important industrial and commercial port with quays taking the largest ships and where transatlantic liners regularly use the harbour. The city also has its own airport serving cross-channel flights, including those of the Aer Lingus car ferry from Bristol and Liverpool.

In the introduction to its town guide, I read "Only a Corkman born and bred can really write about Cork as it deserves to be written about . . ." That lets me out immediately. Especially as, in the next passage, Cork-born writer, the late Robert Gibbings, is quoted as saying: "Cork is the loveliest city in the world. Anybody who doesn't agree with me either was not born there or is prejudiced . . ." I agree with him—at least that it's in the top six!—and I apologise to everyone concerned for the fact that I wasn't born in the city. I shall just have to do my poor best. But it's not much help when Mr. Gibbings—who certainly was prejudiced—takes the words out of your mouth. He said: "The streets are wide, the quays are clean, the bridges are noble. Two wide channels of the river reflect the glittering limestone buildings." Again, I agree—with no need, in a rare case, to allow for his hometown enthusiasm.

He went on to say that Cork is "such a friendly city, too . . . It often seemed that the quickest way to get from one end of Patrick Street to the other, a matter of six hundred yards, would be to take a taxi and tell the driver to make a detour of twenty miles. . . ." Strangers will stop you in the streets and perform all manner of kindnesses, he said. Here I recover my equanimity again, for my wife and boy and I did an extensive walking tour of the city, and so I have two witnesses to prove that not a single Corker did more than glance at us in passing. On second thoughts, Gibbings may still be right. Perhaps no-one liked the look of us.

Much of the city's fascination stems from the fact that it is built on thirteen islands. Consequently, the numerous bridges, together with the quays, underline one of its major characteristics. Also evident on a walking tour—you must do Cork on foot—is the dignity not only of its church and other public buildings, but of those turned over to commercial use as, for instance, in the fine South Mall.

Your sightseeing round should include the open-air market in Cornmarket Street; the river views at one end of the Fitzgerald Park in the Mardyke area; the Georgian houses on Bachelor's Quay; the Shandon Church, architecturally unexceptional, but having an odd "pepper-pot" tower, two sides of limestone, the others of sandstone (you can ascend its 120 feet for a panoramic view of the city); the striking contemporary church of Christ the King at Turner's Cross, designed by a Chicagoan; the partly Romanesque Honan Chapel of the University College; and St. Finbarr's Cathedral, one of the most important examples of early French Gothic style in both Ireland and England.

The University, near the site where Cork originated when St. Finbarr founded his first church and school, has a collection of ogham—ancient Irish burial stones—which visitors can see on request. On display in the Cork Public Museum, where the whole of the city history is depicted, are such arts and crafts as glass, silverware, lace and crochet. Prints of old Cork, contrasted with paintings by modern Cork artists, can also be seen at the Public Library. Contemporary artists are included, too, in the collection of pictures and sculptures open to the public at the School of Art, in Emmet Place.

The same town guide in which Mr. Gibbings tells us how we stand also quotes Thackeray as saying that "the Cork citizens are the most book-loving men I ever met." (I hope this improves my chances, despite Mr. Gibbings.) In fact, I took for granted the existence of a cultural life

114

here as soon as I saw those stately buildings I mentioned. Culture simply oozes from them. Small wonder when you look at the list of groups and societies concerned with such activities. To begin with, there is the Operatic Society. Then come numerous dramatic groups; the Munster Fine Art Society, which holds an annual exhibition of paintings in the School of Art; the Cork Symphony Orchestra; the Cork Orchestral Society; the Irish Theatre Ballet, which is Cork's own professional company making tours throughout the country; the Historical and Archaeological Society; and the Cork Literary and Scientific Society, to which many distinguished archaeologists, explorers, scientists and writers have lectured.

Since it was first held, in 1956, the annual Cork Film Festival, which takes place in September, has acquired a high reputation among the hierarchy of the cinema world. If your visit coincides with the event, you can join, for a fee of $2.40, the Film Festival Club and share its restaurant and bar facilities with the screen stars and directors you will have the opportunity of meeting there. Also important in the Cork calendar is the Summer Show of the Munster Agricultural Society in June. Other summer events, in the city and surrounding country, include regattas and sea angling competitions.

Wherever you go in Ireland, you can usually find excellent meat, poultry and game. Cork and its county, like certain other districts, also serve up fine lobster and other seafood, and salmon and trout from inland waters. If like me you collect cheeses, you will find many in Ireland; among them here in Cork is Blarney, a soft cream cheese which as "that guide" so neatly puts it, is "so persuasive that Blarney was the only name for it!" Another Cork speciality is drisheen, a tasty sort of pudding.

The Buffet Grill in Cook Street is one of the leading

restaurants. Among several of the others in Patrick Street is one called *The Leprechaun*—but I didn't dare go in there! Much of your eating is liable to be done in the *Metropole*, one of the top three hotels, and certainly the most widely-known. It is in the centre of the city although, I thought, not in the most ideal position. You will owe the service and the general pleasure of your stay here—in modern and well-appointed rooms—to the fact that it is run by Mr. Douglas Vance. One of the signs of a good hotel, to me, is a manager or director whom you can always see gliding or darting about the place to ensure that everything is as it should be. Each time I popped into the hotel, and all through the evenings, Mr. Vance was constantly in evidence, wearing an expression of clearly religious fervour in his devotion to the interests of guests. He was the star performer in the star-studded Cork scene.

The other two top-rated hotels are the *Intercontinental*, on Muskerry Island, five minutes from the centre, fifteen from the airport; and the *Imperial* on South Mall.

In and around Patrick Street—without the taxi recommended by Mr. Gibbings!—you will find shops selling all the products for which Ireland has always been noted, including West Cork's own homespun tweeds; tweeds handwoven from millspun yarns; bawneen sweaters; tweed scarves; lightweight stoles; linen; cut-glass from Waterford; Shanagarry pottery; antique silverware; and so on.

Provided you have no particular time limit, you should make Cork your base from which to see the many places of interest nearby. Still within the city is the Marina where, as at the Mardyke, on the south bank of the River Lee, you can enjoy a riverside walk, and beyond which is Blackrock Castle. Montenotte and Tivoli are pleasant residential surburbs of the city, and five miles away is one of the major

116

objectives for all visitors to Ireland—Blarney Castle, five miles from Cork.

The soft-soaping terms in which the Lord of Blarney dealt with her deputy Carew did not fool Queen Elizabeth I. "This is all Blarney!" she declared, and introduced a word the meaning of which the Oxford Dictionary lists as "cajoling talk". Dating from the fifteenth century, the impressive square keep has many window-slits set irregularly without pattern, and an odd protruding balcony. A strange round turret, surmounted by an unexpected porticoed brick section, forms part of the structure, and on either side, there are ruined walls covered in creeper, looking like huge setpieces for an open-air theatre. The performers are the rooks, constantly weaving in and out of the gaping windows, and the whole effect is magnificent.

You need a pocket torch to explore the interior, a copy of the little guide to the castle (on sale at the ticket gate, price 12 c.) and more energy than I have to climb up to the famous Blarney Stone. Those who need the gift of the gab the action is said to bestow on them may here contort themselves to kiss the stone. With or without aid from their escorts, ladies should wear trousers before attempting this feat. Apart from accepting the little folk, I am not otherwise superstitious, so I retained my upright dignity. Anyway, I already talk enough.

Places of interest in the county include Glengariff, Bantry Bay, Kinsale and Ballycotton. Glengariff is reckoned to be one of the country's beauty spots—a small scattered village, set by the sea, in a secluded valley, surrounded by high mountains, with countless islets in its bay, at the entrance of which is the largest and most attractive, Garnish Island. The name means "Island of Holies", and there are here Grecian temples, lily ponds, rock gardens and shrubberies and miniature Japanese trees. You can go

117

there from 10 a.m. to 5.30 p.m. for a landing fee of 30 c.

Glengariff has a mild climate where sub-tropical plants flourish. The warm waters of the Gulf Stream reach its shore. There are several hotels, visitors can bathe safely at numerous coves and inlets, among which are Biddy's Cove, two miles from the village; Poulgorm and Barque Island—these two have diving boards. At the big *Eccles Hotel*, there are salt water baths.

Anglers will find boatmen ready to help them out to the harbour, populated by conger, hake, mackerel, mullet and pollack. The Barony, Counrouska, Eccles and Proudley rivers are good for fresh-water fishing, yielding brown trout, sea trout and salmon, the first of these also being found in various small lakes, especially Barley Lake and Lough Avaul. Fishing in rivers and lakes preserved by the Glengariff Anglers' Club is subject to a small charge for visitors.

Motor and rowboats can be hired for pleasure trips. Other facilities include a nine-hole golf course, mixed shooting—duck, grouse and snipe—which is free, provided the landowners' permission is obtained. Mountain climbers can try the Sugarloaf (1,887 feet) and Gowlbeg (1,178 feet). There are rock-climbing areas around Barley Lake and the Coomarkane Valley, and walks on the ridges of the Caha Mountains.

In Glengariff, you will see handlooms on which Irish tweeds are made—a sign indicates a place where you can buy tweed, and on the left as you approach the village is a cottage with Irish lace on sale. Perched high up on the edge of the bay is the Holy Trinity Church, with a plain glass panel in its stained glass window, through which there is a fine view of the bay. The church also has a simple but colourful altar. Other points of interest for sightseeing are

118

the Megalithic Tomb at Counrouska; the Teampal Fiachna
and nearby, the Petrified Dairy. I must admit I never found
these three places, although several people directed me to
them. Maybe signs have now been put up to help you—if
not, be sure you get a route map.

As at Glengariff, safe bathing, boating, shooting, fresh-
water and sea fishing are features of Bantry, which is
easily reached from Glengariff, but where there are no
top-category hotels. At Kinsale is *Acton's Hotel*, taken over
by the Irish section of Trust Houses, Ltd. in 1962, and
planned to be doubled in size during 1964. Facing the sea,
and with gardens bordering the harbour road, the hotel
makes a good base for quiet holidays where facilities include
what is claimed to be the best sea-angling in Europe
(see page 58), fresh-water fishing, bathing, boating and
golfing.

Kinsale is a picturesque old town, with Georgian houses,
historically interesting churches, and a ruined Carmelite
Friary. Outside the town, there are abbey and castle ruins.
Another castle above the splendid scenery of the Old Head
of Kinsale overlooks the point where the *Lusitania* sank in
1915.

Ballycotton apparently vies with Kinsale as a location for
"some of the finest deep-sea angling in Europe". It is also a
fishing port with a small village, and a resort for the "casual'
type of holiday. There is no sandy beach, but you can swim
from the coves and pools along the shore. Ballycroneen,
six miles west, has a sand beach. Excursions can be made
to Cloyne, seven miles away, to see Cloyne Cathedral, and
the limestone caves on the north side of the village; and,
two miles west, Shanagarry, where there are remains of the
old home of the Penn family, one of whose members
founded the State of Pennsylvania. Two other fishing places
are Cobh, a holiday resort boasting the oldest Yacht Club

in the world, and Crosshaven, near which are some interesting castles and the wooded creek of Drake's Pool, where, in 1587, Sir Francis, pursued by a larger Spanish fleet, hid with five of the ships under his command.

CORK TO KILLARNEY

If you happen to make Blarney Castle your first excursion of the day following your stay in Cork, and you are heading for Killarney, you need not come back into the city after seeing the castle. Head for Macroom, to which the signs are clearly marked. Along this road, I drove through hedgerows bright with orange montbretia, and saw quaint gypsy caravans, several small, unnamed lakes, and a pack of hounds being exercised by two men on bicycles. In Macroom, on a Thursday morning, there was a horse market in progress. Beyond the town, the road is still quite good, though less smooth than the stretch from Cork, and more winding. Heather-covered crags are a feature of the interesting scenery from here.

I have always hesitated before describing certain places on the international tourist beat which are world-famous for their beauty. Invariably, this has been recorded so well by many writers that all I can do is follow in the footsteps and inkmarks of the masters. Sometimes, when the places are added to my short list of favourites, I feel less inadequate. In Killarney, I was excused by the Tourist Board literature, which claims that so many changes occur there almost hourly that "poets, painters and writers have never fully succeeded in conveying the varied beauty of form and colour of this wonderland of mountains and lakes." Thus released of my obligations, I will begin simply by saying that Killarney rapidly took a high place in the list, and is now contesting with several spots in Italy as the one to which I shall hie me when I am ready to face the final judgment. Killarney has an advantage over the others. It has been called "Heaven's Reflex". This encourages its use as a settlement for earthly sinners, who may reasonably expect to be dealt with leniently when they get there.

It was a good thing I saw Killarney when I did, because I found the view of the Middle Lake from Muckross House is the most peacemaking I have ever seen—and, of course, it will take years of persuasion before the authorities will let me live there, periodically and at the crucial period. If I succeed in this aim, but not in reaching heaven, then at least I shall have seen, from those windows, something of what it may be like there. Readers inspired by these thoughts please note I have already staked my claim with the National Trust of Ireland.

The house is not open to visitors, some of whom, when it was, caused damage to the property. But you can roam round the extensive grounds—wooded, yet interspersed with well-kept lawns. There is also a magnificent rockery. From the terrace at the side of the house, you can stand and look at that view over the Middle Lake—sometimes called Torc or Muckross Lake—which, instead of describing it, I will leave you to judge for yourself.

The Muckross Estate, presented to the Irish Government by Mr. and Mrs. William Bowers Bourn of California, and their son-in-law, Mr. Arthur Vincent, is in effect a 10,000-acre national park containing most of the Killarney Lake District. There are deer in the park. But no birds sing. Even they are anxious not to disturb "Heaven's Reflex".

Caves and all kinds of odd shapes can be seen in the limestone eroded by the waters around the Lower and Middle Lakes. Lough Leane, the Lower Lake, is separated from the Middle Lake by the wooded Muckross peninsula.

121

The Upper Lake is joined by the Long Range, a narrow strait, also wooded. In fact, the lakes are surrounded by woods, and they lie in a valley between red sandstone mountains with rich, craggy names—Bennaunmore, Crohane, Stoompa, Esduff, Mangerton, Torc, Cromaglan and MacGillycuddy's Reeks. In this last range is the top peak for climbers, Carrantuohill (3,414 feet) the highest in Ireland.

As the Tourist Board's official guide to Kerry contains a very clear and comprehensive section on Killarney, I recommend you to use this if you are planning a lengthy stay. No-one should hurry away from what is one of the few places where, even if you cannot stop the clock, at least you can live for a while at the relaxed pace we were really meant to maintain. Do this, for instance, with Larry O'Rourke, driver of one of the jaunting-cars on which you sit, almost side-saddle in effect, watching the glorious scenery unfurl slowly before you. Larry and the horse, Willie, were a perfect team. I hope they are still together, so that when you hire them to take you through the park and alongside the lakes Larry, instead of rattling off information coldly like many coach-tour guides, will tell you just enough to match the tempo of the ride, and Willie will impress you when, rather than trot down the far side of a rise in the pathway as you may see other horses do, he brakes down gently, without any help from Larry. Even if you don't find Larry and Willie, you are bound to have an enjoyable trip—the length of which can be varied to suit you.

Apart from Muckross House, places to see include the Meeting of the Waters (of the Middle and Upper Lakes), Torc Waterfall, Ross Castle, the Gap of Dunloe and Kate Kearney's Cottage. In the Lower Lake, Innisfallen Island, with the ruined abbey near its landing-stage, is one of the places to which boat-trips can be made. Another way of keeping to the leisurely life in Killarney is by hiring one of the bicycles which are available for touring. You can also make certain trips on the back of a pony. Other peaceful pursuits here in "wonderland" are mountain-climbing, golf, tennis, fishing, shooting and (by special arrangement with the Office of Public Works in Dublin) deer-stalking. It would be unseemly to ask for more!

Killarney offers a wide choice of hotels. I am very partial to the Great Southern Hotels, run by C.I.E., Ireland's Transport Company, and although the one at Killarney has much in common with its counterparts elsewhere, I found its public rooms rather busy. This, the only unrelaxing note in becalmed Killarney, may not be confined to the *Great Southern*—and, I suppose is an unavoidable penalty on the magnetic district! The hotel actually is a fine, big place, with extremely comfortable rooms. It has a grill room, restaurant (and fishpool from which you can select your own trout); cocktail bar; hairdressing salon and a six-hour laundry and valet service; a very well-stocked shop selling Irish craft products; large grounds; its own fleet of boats and its own jaunting cars—it was here that I discovered Larry and Willie. And on a fire-escape facing my window, there was a splendid peacock, looking rather like a James Bond character, obviously sent by the "little people" to watch over my interests.

The *Lake Hotel* is probably well-known to English visitors. It has a fine position at the water's edge, enabling guests not only to enjoy the view, but also to bathe safely off its pier, or further along the shore. Outstandingly good and on the lake, too, is the *Castlerosse* and among other leading hotels are the *Europe*, the *International* and the *Arbutus*—this last is a modest pleasant family hotel. I also liked the look of the *Gleneagle* by Castlelough Bay, and the

123

gay little *Whitegates* guest house run by Mr. and Mrs. Bill Turner.

At Glenflesk, on nearby Lough Guitane, and on your way in from Macroom on the Cork road, is the *Curraglass Inn*, behind which you can see the ruined home of the O'Donoghue Kings.

THE RING OF KERRY

Whether or not you feel like detaching yourself from Killarney, which is most unlikely, you should stay there long enough to use it as a base for seeing the Ring of Kerry. Drive out on the north side of Lough Leane to Killorglin. This is the place where the "Puck Fair" is held in August and a couple of miles to the west is Ballykissane Pier. Here, four volunteers on their way to Dublin by car in 1916, took the wrong road and drove off the pier into the sea, becoming the first casualties of the Rising. On their way to make contact with Sir Roger Casement and the "Aud", bringing arms to Ireland, three of them were drowned, and are commemorated by a monument on the pier.

Next comes Glenbeigh, in a splendid mountain setting. There is an interesting ruin called "Wynne's Folly" near the village, and the *Towers Hotel* helps to make this a good base for fishing, golfing, riding and trekking holidays. The hotel actually organises special holidays on horseback in April and May, late September and October. You can ride through mountain passes and alongside the lake, tuition is given on a four-mile beach at Rossbeigh, and the long day in the open-air is broken by tea served at a farmhouse by an open peat fire. The inclusive daily rate for the six-day horseback holiday is $8.40 per person.

From Glenbeigh, the road winds along the coast overlooking Dingle Bay towards Cahirciveen. On my journey,

124

as elsewhere in the country, I saw donkey carts being used for collections from the peat seams. Time is of very little consequence wherever you go in a sensible country like Ireland, but if you want to visit one of the places in which it virtually stands still, take a trip to Valentia Island while you can, from Cahirciveen. You won't be able to disturb the peace of the privileged folk who have found themselves an "away-from-it-all" haven here, because the former *Royal Hotel* has been turned into a guest house which carefully coddles its residents by refusing to serve those who are not staying there. If you can't fight 'em, you should join 'em, in which case you will probably be so content that you may not see the rest of Ireland, especially as the hotel brochure states "garage on mainland".

The island is about seven miles long and three miles wide, has a population of roughly a thousand. Sub-tropical plants and trees have grown here, among them the largest fuchsia in the world. Beginish Strand and other neighbouring islands can be visited by motor-boat, and there is excellent deep-sea fishing in the local waters. The remains of a beehive monastery can be seen on Church Island in Valentia Harbour, and there are other beehive dwellings, also believed to have been inhabited by fifth- and sixth-century monks, on the Skelligs Rock, fifteen miles away. Little Skelligs, alongside the bigger rock, is one of Europe's three gannet sanctuaries, and the second largest in the world. Other places of interest are the subterranean Cathedral Cave by Doulus Head, and Ballycarbery Castle. Near Knightstown, the island "capital", one of the disused slate quarries has been converted into a Lourdes grotto, with a water cascade, fountain and altar. A ferry service is operated between the island and the mainland slipway at Reenard during the summer season. The fare is 12 c.

The European end of the Western Union Telegraph

Company's Atlantic Cable is on Valentia, and in 1859, two years after the cable was laid, a detailed map of the island was produced. A printed note on the map, at the location of the *Royal*, reads: "Pronounced by the Right Hon. Lord John Manners, M.P., as the neatest, cleanest and most comfortable little hotel in all Ireland." Over a century later, in a bigger, even more comfortable and modernised building, the management claims to carry on in the same tradition.

Continuing round the Ring, you come to Waterville, a famous angling centre set on the narrow strip of land which separates the sea from Lough Currane, one of the most beautiful lakes in the country. You can bathe from a very good sandy beach, and there is a nine-hole golf course. I recommend you to lunch or stay at the *Butler Arms Hotel*, another of the places well-known to English visitors. Owner William Huggard was not available when I was there but his kindly staff made it quite clear to me why the hotel is so popular. It is a family hotel, and Waterville is a place in which to have a holiday with a "growing-up" family, one where its younger members can enjoy spending the time in outdoor activity, constantly renewed by the excellent fuel in the hotel dining-room. A games room takes care of them when the weather is unkind. Hotel visitors have free salmon and trout fishing on Lough Currane, and several small brown trout lakes and rivers. There is also reserve fishing on the Waterville River.

Magnificent coastal scenery opens up as you move on round the Ring from Waterville, and you will see many attractive coves with sandy beaches. I drove down to inspect some of them, passing hedgerows laden with tiger lilies, and I stopped to ask a local woman whether children could safely bathe from the coves. She assured me they could, also telling me that the mean little building generating a noise like something out of "Quatermass" which stood in one of the coves was "Lucie's lobster pond". Such an eyesore making such a row in this lovely place gave me visions of the seafood delicacy-holder grown to awful science-fictional size, so I dared not ask her for more details.

Looking upon caravans, too, as one of many inventions of the devil, I shuddered again when I returned to the main road and saw there were sites to let just before the Derrynane headland. Here, incidentally, there are signposts to the beaches, $1\frac{1}{4}$ miles down, and the biggest of which can be seen from the top road. A few miles further on, you will see a silver sand beach near the road, and another unsecluded caravan site.

As you approach Sneem, the scenery changes again, to a panorama of the now distant mountains, and just beyond Sneem is another of the places long-favoured by British tourists—Parknasilla, with another of the excellent Great Southern Hotels. Being only thirty miles from Killarney, it makes a good centre for touring that area, too. The hotel stands in a fine 200-acre estate on the shore of the Kenmare river, and has its own motor launch for cruising round the little islands in the bay. Other amenities include a nine-hole golf course, tennis courts, shooting, sea and river angling. Indoor attractions include dancing and film shows. Restaurant meals are interchangeable with the other Great Southern Hotels.

Beyond Parknasilla is the pleasant Tahilla Cove guest house and in Kenmare, where I arrived on a Thursday afternoon to find a sheep market in progress, there is yet another of the Great Southern Hotels. It has all the facilities of the one at Parknasilla and, like that and the others on the circuit, one of those useful shops in the foyer selling Irish craft products. The *Kenmare Hotel* also has woodland gardens.

Kenmare has an annual regatta in August, and apart from boat trips on the river, there is plenty to do here, including bathing and fishing, shooting, golf, and riding. Using Kenmare as yet another alternative base, you can also go climbing in the Killarney mountains and other nearby ranges I have mentioned. A mile out of the town are the Sheen Falls. Kenmare lace is world-famous—it is made at the Convent of the Poor Clares. If you have not already visited Glengariff, you can conveniently do so from Kenmare, travelling on a road which goes through rugged scenery. Beyond the last of several rock tunnels, there is the unusual sight, on the right, of a lake on high level. And if you are returning to Killarney from Kenmare, you will see a view of its lakes on your left, set amid the majestic mountains. You will also pass isolated shops selling tweeds, and a ruined tower on the right.

Tralee, north-west of Killarney, is a modern town with no special pretensions to being a tourist attraction, but it is well-known through the song, "The Rose of Tralee", written by William Mulchinock, who was born and died there. The famous American baseball player, Roger Bresnahan, who invented shinguards, was also a native of the town.

Rounding off in County Kerry, if you have more than the average amount of time to spare, go further north of Tralee, and north-west of Listowel to Ballybunion. Alternatively, if you like the bracing kind of air that comes in from the Atlantic here, stay and enjoy it in this holiday resort, which has numerous hotels and is only nine miles from Listowel. The tall cliffs of Ballybunion contain at their foot many caves, romantically thought to have been smugglers' haunts. Some are accessible on foot, others only by boat but still for a considerable distance after leaving the open sea. There is some impressive rock scenery at Doon Bay, an inlet one

13. The Cliffs of Moher, Co. Clare

14.   Aran Island currachs

15.   Roundstone Harbour, Co. Galway, with the Twelve Bens in the background

mile northward, and the remains of Ballybunion Castle can be seen on the headland between the two parts of the strand. Lick Castle ruins are also nearby. Close to the village of Ballyduff, five miles south, is the Round Tower of Rattoo, one of the most perfect specimens in the country. Back towards Tralee, actually twenty-two miles away from Ballybunion, is Ardfert, worth visiting to see the ruined cathedral.

LIMERICK

Limerick, chief town of County Limerick, is the third largest city in Ireland. It is historically and industrially important, has also become a key transport centre through the development of nearby Shannon Airport, and is close to the Shannon Hydro-Electric Station at Ardnacrusha. The city is famed for its fine lace and lovely women, also—if one can mention it in the same breath—its bacon!

The treaty of 1691 guaranteeing religious freedom to Irish Catholics was repudiated by the English Parliament and earned for Limerick the title "City of the Violated Treaty". It is believed that the stone which rests on a pedestal at one end of Thomond Bridge is that on which the Treaty was signed. Among other sights to see are King John's Castle, built in 1210; the old city walls; St. Mary's Cathedral and many other churches, only to be expected in this great religious centre. The Art Gallery and Museum contains modern Irish paintings and historically interesting objects including a pedestal called the "Nail" on which, when it stood outside the now ruined Exchange building in Nicholas Street, Limerick merchants used to pay their debts. This is the origin of the expression "paying on the nail".

Although lace-making is mainly an industry carried on in

homes, it can be seen at the Good Shepherd Convent in Clare Street. A particularly interesting excursion can be made to Lough Gur, twelve miles south of the city and a quarter-mile east of the Limerick–Kilmallock road. The lake shores are lined with many ancient monuments—stone circles and forts, dolmens and other megalithic tombs, the whole of the excavations giving evidence of continuous occupation from neolithic to late medieval times. The remains of extinct animals have also been unearthed in caves above the lake.

In this quiet, pleasant county, among other things to see are the well-kept ruins of the thirteenth-century Dominican Abbey near Kilmallock and, in that town, the King's Castle, also in a good state of preservation; the big, red sandstone, roofless church in the little village of Bally-landers, near Kilfinane—it was left unfinished in the seventeenth century; the ruins of Rathmore Castle at Croom; the thatched houses, lichen-covered churches and Abbey at Adare; the ruined Desmond Castle; and the cloisters—I always find those fascinating—at Askeaton Abbey. Of hotels at which to stay in Limerick itself, *Cruise's* and the *Royal George*, both in O'Connell Street, are among the well-known ones. Intercontinental Group also has a hotel in the city, five minutes from the centre, and fifteen miles from Shannon Airport.

Only six miles from Limerick, as you move on into Clare County, is Bunratty Castle. The road is quite wide at this point, and you are liable to be travelling quite fast but, like me, you will probably find it necessary to slow down as your attention is drawn to the tall, rectangular, mainly fifteenth-century structure. It is even more striking because it shares the limelight with the *Shannon Shamrock Inn*, a low-built contemporary hotel which stands alongside.

The castle has been restored and furnished as it was when

the Earl of Thomond lived there, and visitors can dine like that lord, at his table, drinking mead from a posset cup and toasts in claret as he did in the fifteenth century. To enjoy this medieval banquet, advance reservations are essential and can be made up to 3.30 p.m. on any day for the banquet of that evening, or by telephoning (Shannon Airport 291) or writing to the manager of the castle. When you arrive, Irish girls in medieval costumes greet you with the "bread of friendship", serve you with the banquet and then sing songs of ancient heroes. The charge, including food, wine, entertainment and entrance fees, is $4.20.

During the day, the castle, first built by the Norman invaders, makes a most interesting excursion tour. It stands on what used to be an island called Tradree on the north shore of the Shannon and, up to the end of the eighteenth century, was washed by the tide, and accessible only by a track from the old Limerick road. I liked the chapels, the Earl's bedroom, and his kitchen with its early type rubbish chute—a hole in the wall which took refuse down to the foundations and away into the river. Under the great banqueting hall is another hall with a shop, from which you can buy a very interesting little booklet-guide to the castle. In this room, a big Irish wolfhound sleeps on a huge wooden-framed palliasse. Mulled claret is served in one of the halls.

The castle is among the places visited on a one-day Medieval Tour operated from Shannon Airport for passengers in transit either to Europe or America. Neither they nor holidaymakers can fail to be intrigued by the specimen menu of the banquet: "First Remove"—Vegetable Bruse; "Second Remove"—Stuffed Boar's Head, Petty Toes in Gellye, Beef Ryall, Pull'd Fowl-Salamagundy; and "Third Remove"—Everlasting Syllabubs (with of course, good measure of mead and claret).

The banquet comes at the end of the tour which leaves Shannon at times to suit the arrival of either eastbound or westbound passengers, and begins with tea before a turf fire in a thatched cottage at Bunratty; goes on through Cratloe Forest to the old-world village of Sixmilebridge, Gallows Hill and the twelfth-century Quin Abbey. Following a tour of the Abbey, there is a display of Irish dancing at a hotel in Ennis, and the coach then returns to Bunratty through Dromoland, Clarecastle and Newmarket-on-Fergus. Westbound passengers have a chance to see Limerick city, and everyone has the opportunity of shopping in the duty-free shop at the airport. The cost of the one-day tour, including transport, meals, entertainment and accommodation at Shannon Airport is five guineas ($12.60). Reservations can be made before leaving home, through travel agents.

The *Shannon Shamrock Inn* makes a good base for touring the area; for fishing on Lough Derg and in the Mulcaire river; for golfing on two eighteen-hole courses not more than 35 minutes away by car, or on championship courses at Lahinch (see page 136) and Killarney (see page 120); for rough shooting and hunting. The hotel is 15 minutes drive from Shannon, 15 minutes from Limerick, and 30 minutes from Ennis (see below). All rooms have private bathrooms and some have connecting doors for family use. The lounge, cocktail bar and restaurant are all very attractive, and there is a swimming pool outside the building. Many of the places already mentioned and some of those in the following pages can be visited while staying at the inn.

ENNIS

On the way to Galway, I headed for Ennis, to stop at the *Old Ground*, yet another of the hotels well-known to British visitors. Manager Jack Donnelly gave me a big welcome and the recipe for Irish Coffee, which you will find on page 45. At the bottom of the printed slip is what is described as "Old Irish Toast" and headed: SLAINTE!! (Good Health). Below are these words:

> Health and long life to you
> Land without rent to you
> A child every year to you
> And may you die in Ireland.

The motto of the O'Regan family who have owned the hotel for many years is "Mullach Abu"—On Top Forever— and the strange name of the hotel originated long ago when it was the home of a great Clare family, the O'Gorman Mahon, and passed by inheritance to a distant relative. On his arrival to take up residence, he was warmly greeted by an old retainer with the words "You are welcome to the old ground, sir." Because they were said with much emotion, the young owner called his home "The Old Ground" and the hotel staff still welcome guests in the same way.

You will find the hotel easily in the centre of Ennis, the county town of Clare. This is a small, quiet place of only 6,000 inhabitants, and although it has little to occupy visitors' interest, I certainly sensed its friendliness, and was delighted with a piece in its guide-booklet which, under the heading "Us and our Narrow Streets", reads as follows:

"It is difficult to know whether or not to tell you that we like our town. If you are only a passing motorist in a hurry and caught in a jam in one of our narrow streets we fear your verdict may not be favourable; however, if you can tarry a while with us you will see we have much in common. Our narrow streets slow *us* down also and it is possibly this which is responsible for a very noticeable slowing of the tempo of modern living which exasperates foreigners but which becomes infectious if lived in for a short time. Yes, we get caught in traffic jams daily but this gives us infinite patience and possibly makes us walk where you would drive.*

"Our houses are close together and higgledy piggledy but this makes us more neighbourly and yet different. Our streets amble along the banks of a lazy river and perhaps we do also but you can take my word for it that the waters of that river still reach the sea and then it is not just any sea but the mighty Atlantic Ocean.

"Of course not all of our town has narrow streets. We have our new housing estates and modern factories, stately public buildings and modern hotels, but we have in our narrow streets that link with the past, which in us gives a blending of new and old which we like and which seemingly others like—and we hope that includes you.

"Should we pull down those narrow streets and build a broad highway to speed the motorist on his way? (Incidentally, I am sure he is still stuck in that traffic jam.) You say No. We thought so. Welcome to Ennis—come and meet us. Tell at your hotel, at the tourist bureau or in any shop, that you would wish to meet someone in your profession, trade or line of business and they will be only too willing to arrange this for you. I guess I was right in telling you to judge us by our town after all."

The Irish, a rural race, used not to live in towns, rather, from the time of St. Patrick, in settlements in and around monasteries. There were five such settlements within six miles of the present town, at the abbeys of Ennis, Clare, Drumcliffe (the first to be founded), Killone and Quin.

* In fact, by our standards, the jams are negligible.

134

The ruins of both Ennis Abbey and Quin Abbey should be seen, even if you are not staying but merely passing through. Of Ennis Abbey, one historian has said: "There is no more elegant structure in these islands." According to another writer: "the glorious east window of Ennis Abbey is a gem studded with gems" and another wrote: "Through the iron gate separating the ageless ruins from our everyday streets, the eye travels along the grass-carpeted gracious nave, long and high, to the glory of the great east window. No longer do its slender mullion and lofty lancets hold the rich blue glass of which the chroniclers wrote 'its only blue now is the sudden gleam of a spring day behind the stone lacery'."

Still standing in the ruins is the Royal Tomb, thought to be one of the finest monuments of its time. Cromwell's troops scattered sections of the tomb, but the panels which were found intact were replaced in their correct position a hundred years ago. Preserved on the tomb are fine grey marble panels depicting Passion and Resurrection. On top is a great bearded Christ. The key of the Abbey is obtainable from Mulqueen's Shop adjoining the grounds.

Ennis town grew in importance during the time of James I who granted its Charter giving the right to hold fairs and markets and collect taxes. James II granted another Charter making Ennis a borough, and in the records of the period, the only council official described in detail was the beadle or night watchman. He was dressed in a blue cloth coat faced with red cloth, blue trews, yellow yarn stockings, a bright red hat with a wide brim around which was white worsted lace; and in his hand he carried a yellow staff.

The town gave birth to some famous people, among them artist William Mulready, some of whose pictures hang in London, Paris and Rome galleries, and who designed the first penny postage envelope issued by Rowland Hill, the inventor of the penny postage; and the nineteenth-century actress Harriet Constance Smithson, who married the French composer, Hector Berlioz.

LAHINCH

Through Ennistymon—look for the unusual, dark-grey towered church—I came to Lahinch. This particular journey was made when the main trunk telephone service was strikebound and before I left the *Old Ground*, Jack Donnelly had insisted on ringing through to the *garda* station and asking the police there to tell Michael Vaughan, of *Vaughan's Hotel*, that I was coming. The hotel is famous for its food, Mr. Vaughan for his fund of Irish stories, some true, others question-markable! Ask him to tell you the one about the American millionaire, and the one about the old woman who was almost buried alive.

As soon as I arrived, Mr. Vaughan stopped looking after his hotel to guide me on the short drive to the wonderful Cliffs of Moher. Six miles north-west of the town, they stretch for almost five miles, from Hag's Head (440 feet) to O'Brien's Tower where they rise to nearly 700 feet. A fort after which the cliffs were named once stood on Hag's Head, where there are now the ruins of a watch tower built as part of the coastal defences at the time of the Napoleonic invasion. O'Brien's Tower, a round, castle-like structure, was built in 1835, by Cornelius O'Brien, an M.P. and local landowner "who built everything around here except the cliffs" and who intended it as a viewpoint for them. In fact, it is the best and usual place from which to look.

A signpost at the roadside points the way to the cliff edge, within a few feet of which you can take your car on a specially constructed road, and there is a safety wall for quite a way along the cliffs. They are, of course, very impressive.

Lahinch, which lies on the shore of Liscannor Bay, is a small but very attractive resort, with a fine mile-long sandy beach, and its eighteen-hole golf course is a well-known championship venue. Long ago, Lahinch was surrounded by water on two sides, and known for this reason as "Half Island" and its present name, meaning O'Connor's Cairn, derives from the fact that an important member of the O'Connor family is buried there.

Bathing huts can be hired on the beach, and a life guard is on duty during the summer months. *Vaughan's Hotel* will provide surf-boards—the sea is ideal—and boating enthusiasts can hire *curraghs* at Liscannor, three miles away, and there are boats available on the River Inagh at Ennistymon, two miles away. The Inagh, and the Dealagh river offer good brown trout fishing. So do Doo Lough (nine miles south), Inchiquin Lake (twelve miles east), Lickeen Lake (five miles north-east) and Rockmount Lake (six miles south). Salmon are also found, as well as some sea trout in the autumn. Grey mullet and bass can be caught in the estuaries of the two rivers, and there is sea-fishing, for herring, mackerel and pollack, in Liscannor Bay. The area also offers good duck and snipe shooting.

In the little fishing village of Liscannor, on the northern shore of the bay, three miles north-west of Lahinch, are the ruins of an O'Connor castle, later won from them by the O'Briens, and close by, in Castle Street, is the house in which John P. Holland, inventor of the submarine, was born. Two miles north-west of Liscannor is St. Brigid's Well, the waters of which are said to be curative, and to which pilgrimages are made in the summer.

Ten miles north of Lahinch is Lisdoonvarna, the curative waters of which have made it Ireland's chief spa. There are

137

both sulphur and iron springs here. Local points of interest are Ballynalacken Castle, a fifteenth-century O'Brien stronghold; Doonagore Castle, a first-class specimen of the round type of castle, overlooking Ballaghaline Bay; Corcomroe Abbey and Kilfenora Cathedral; and Ballykinvarga Caher, one of a series of stone forts.

Lisdoonvarna is at the edge of the fascinating Burren country, a great stretch of denuded limestone in north-western Clare, on the southern shore of Galway Bay. The Burren—the name means "big rock"—is an area almost without water, and devoid of soil except between cracks in the limestone, yet the amount of flora which grows there is remarkable. There are anemones; mountain avens; spring gentian, brightly blue; the eye-catching "bloody cranesbill"; orchids; maidenhair fern and saxifrage. The flora is at its best in the early part of summer.

Entomologists will find plenty of insect life, including some species they have probably not discovered elsewhere. From every point of view, much of the region has yet to be explored fully, even the archaeological remains not being completely listed. Wherever you go in the Burren, you will see prehistoric remains. There are some 700 stone forts, and a great many dolmens. Among the latter is an unusual double dolmen at Baur, near Noughaval. Little ruined churches of the sixth century, and plain stone altars can be seen.

Corcomroe Abbey, near Bell Harbour on Galway Bay, is one of the monastic foundations which grew up here in later Christian times. It contains the tomb of King Conor O'Brien, with the "smiling bishop" effigy above, some fine carvings and an amazingly tall east window. Apart from the chancel, the building is roofless.

You may be lucky enough to find the treasure in the Burren. This happened to a boy out rabbiting with his dog, one day in 1938. The dog, pawing away at a burrow when a rabbit went to ground, dug up a strange object which the boy examined and found to be a circular piece of metal, shaped as a flat collar, and ornamented with rows of beading. It was a solid gold gorget, undiscovered for over 2,000 years and undamaged.

Many other interesting finds were made in one of the numerous caves in the Burren. The caves are easy to explore, and the longest system is that of Pollnaglollum east of Slieve Elva Hill, west of which and also worth exploring are Faunarooska and the Polldubh system. South of the hill are the Coolagh river cave and the Doolin system. Altogether, there are 25 miles of cave passages. In the lowland area north-eastwards to Gort, there is a complex system of lakes, some with underground links, and many (called turloughs) which disappear overnight, as well as streams which disappear into potholes.

Various Burren legends have been woven around Leminagh Castle, a stronghold of the O'Briens, particularly about Maire Ruadh, who ruled from the castle three hundred years ago. In order to retain her lands and power, she married an English officer, and quickly rid herself of him. According to one story, she was walled up alive in Bunratty Castle, and still "walks" there—although other opinion deems it unlikely that anyone would have had the temerity to do this to her.

Another story of her death, told in more recent times, is that when riding her black stallion to Limerick, she passed a ramshackle house by the roadside, which she said offended her and was to be demolished before she passed that way again. The poor woman who lived in the house watched the retreating figure on the black horse and, falling on her bare knees in the road, cursed Maire Ruadh, that she might never ride back that way. As the lady on the black horse passed through the woods of Cratloe, a great wind rose. A branch of a tree was bent down and caught Maire Ruadh by the throat. Her neck was broken. On a stormy night, it is said, you can hear the heavy feet of the stallion, galloping on the road up to Leminagh.

Elsewhere in County Clare, there is much to see, and among worthwhile places at which to stay are the *Lakeside Hotel* at Killaloe on Lough Derg, where guests can become members of the water-ski club—the hotel introduced water-skiing to Ireland—and where you can also enjoy fishing, pony riding and various sports; and Dromoland Castle, another former O'Brien home, now converted into a luxury hotel offering salmon and trout fishing, wild goose and duck shooting, snipe bogs, sailing, water-skiing, tennis courts and an eighteen-hole championship golf course.

The west coast resort of Kilkee has a sandy beach with safe bathing, boating, fishing, golfing and shooting facilities. It also has a great deal of attractive cliff scenery, caves and the Loop Head Peninsula, to the south-west, makes a very pleasant and interesting excursion. One of the things to see is "the Little Ark" in the church of Moneen. In 1850, the people of the district were refused land on which to build a church, but the parish priest, Father Michael Meehan, helped by the people built a hut on wheels, in which Mass was celebrated for more than six years. The "Ark" used to be wheeled on to the shore between high and low tides.

GALWAY

Most people I have discussed it with—Irish and visitors—share my liking for the town of Galway. I am a long way behind the first writer to mention it—Ptolemy in 2 A.D. But it was then called Magnata, and Galway was actually founded in 1124, became a Norman town in 1228. In the fourteenth, fifteenth and part of the sixteenth centuries, it was an independent state, only subject to the Kings of England.

An Anglo-Norman colony grew up and gave birth to the "Tribes of Galway"—families which included the Blakes, Bodkins, Brownes, D'Arcys, ffrenches, Kirwans, Joyces, Lynches, Martins, Morrisses and Skerrets. The settlers kept themselves apart from the local people, and a bye-law of 1518 laid down "that neither O nor Mac shall strutte ne swagger thro' the streets of Galway." Despite this, the natives often succeeded in raiding the town, and at one period the West Gate bore the inscription "From the fury of the O'Flahertys good Lord deliver us."

Richard II gave the town a royal charter in 1396, and this was confirmed during successive reigns. Trade first with Italy and France and later with Spain helped to establish Galway as an important commercial centre, and the Spanish influence remains in some of the architecture, to a lesser extent in the people and their dress.

The city went into decline when Elizabeth I came to the throne and remained in that state for more than two hundred years. Today, it is again a thriving commercial and educational centre—it has a university—also, as the capital of Connacht, an administrative centre. It is a good base from which to tour Loughs Corrib and Mask, the lovely Connemara country, parts of County Clare and the Aran Islands.

Whether or not they had this last aspect in mind, the C.I.E. people have set up, overlooking the big, wide bay about which the song was written, the *Great Southern*— not only one of the finest hotels in all Ireland, but a highly-placed favourite on the international list of those to which I have travelled. While most of the windows look on to the bay, the entrance is in Eyre Square, named after a mayor

141

who presented it to the town in 1710. The late President Kennedy was made a Freeman of Galway in the square in 1963. The casket which contained the freedom scroll was of solid silver on a base of Connemara marble, and it was supplied by Stephen Faller, the jeweller, in Williamsgate, to whose principal Mr. Cornelius Faller I am grateful for permission to include certain facts from his own little guide to the town.

By the time you read this, a plan I heard about may have been completed—the railings around the square will have disappeared, making the little park more attractive. There was talk of installing a swimming pool, too. I have stayed at the *Great Southern* on more than one occasion, and I always felt it to be a happy hotel, where the traditional welcome of Ireland is at its best, with an attentive and kindly staff, a really fine atmosphere, beautifully-appointed rooms, and some of the best food you can find.

This last, especially in the rooftop *Claddagh Grill*, is due to livewire restaurant manager Bernie Casey, assisted by wine-waiter Danny Lydon, far famed expert at making Irish coffee to his own improved recipe. In this room, let me stress, I have eaten the best smoked eel of all time— it comes, like the fine salmon, from the local waters, in the River Corrib weir, where you can see the salmon jumping at the appropriate season. There is a big bar on the daïs at one end of the grill room, with the chef's dispensary facing it, all of which, plus the excellent service, gives the room wonderful atmosphere.

On the *Claddagh Grill* menu, you can read the following piece: "In the seventeenth century a seafaring Youth, one Joyce, fell into the hands of a band of Pirates or Sea Robbers from that part of the North of Africa which adjoins the Sea. Having bound him, they bore him away to languish in Captivity in their chief City, called Tunis.

142

In which City he did learn of Precious Metals, of gold and of the beating of Silver. And so it was until the time in 1689 that King William III of England effected a Compact with the Moors whereby all his Subjects in captivity were set at Liberty. Joyce's master held him in exceeding high regard and offered him the hand of his Daughter in Marriage if he would continue in his Service. But Joyce, yearning to once more see his erstwhile home, straightly embraced the Ransom of the King. Thus it was that Joyce, after many Voyagings came home to Galway. And Men say that it was this Joyce who first fashioned the Claddagh Ring with the Joined Hands of Friendship; and to signify Human Charity, the Heart of Man. Greatly indeed were these Claddagh Rings treasured by the Women of the Claddagh, who wore them in Marriage, and bequeathed them at Death."

Not content with their splendid achievements in the grill room, the hotel management has by now opened new restaurants on the ground floor—the Rose Room and the Oyster Room—which were nearing completion at the time of my last visit. You will also find there is a new bar, called Cois Farraige (by the sea) in which the speaking of Irish is the aim, although those who only have English are also welcome! There is another big bar on the ground floor, and a gift shop alongside. Two other things worth mentioning are the Irish entertainments put on in the season, and one of which I was very impressed with on my first visit here; and the fact that, if you are interested, the hotel has some lock-up garages.

Much of the credit for the success of this hotel which I cannot praise too highly is due to the manager, smiling and relaxed Brendan Maher, and his assistant, Mr. Murphy. Irish charm is typified by Mr. Maher, the sort the ladies appreciate and film directors contract on a long-term basis. One of the latter, John Huston, lives in Galway part of his

143

time, and if he has tried to win over Brendan Maher he has failed because there is obviously more of a challenge and greater satisfaction in keeping this admirable hotel where it is!

In the corner of the square to the left of the hotel as you come out, is the National Bank, where, in a glass showcase, Galway keeps its historic sword and mace. The sword dates from the time of the charter of King James I which, in 1610, gave authority for such a weapon to be carried before the Mayor. Silver-mounted and richly ornamented, it bears marks identified as those of Galway silversmiths. The mace, nearly five feet long, was made in Dublin in 1710 and presented to the town by Edward Eyre—the mayor I have mentioned already—in 1712. The whole of its surface is decorated with engraved, chased and embossed designs of foliage, scrollwork and classical figures. For some time during the period when the town had no corporation—1841 to 1937—the sword and mace were out of the town, and were presented to Galway in 1960 by the Hearst Foundation of America, having been housed previously at St. Donat's Castle, near Cardiff.

On the same side of the square as the National Bank is the *Skeffington Arms Hotel* where the bar is quite a social centre of the town and which, like the *Odeon Hotel* on the opposite side, is very modern. Another good hotel is *Ardilaun House*, in its own grounds one mile from the town centre and half-a-mile from Salthill, the Galway seaside resort. Galway Golf Club and Tennis Club are also nearby. The Browne Doorway, bearing the Spanish influence, and the monument to the great Gaelic writer Padraic O Conaire, round off the points of interest in the square.

Coming out of the north side of the square into the shopping centre, you can begin sightseeing on a pleasant little tour that will not tire you. On the right, in Shop Street, is the Lynch Castle, a mansion dating from 1320, much restored and now a bank. Gothic in style, its façade bears typically Irish ornamentation, and the arms of Henry VIII. Continue along Shop Street and turn into Lombard Street, where the St. Nicholas Collegiate Church stands. This too, dates from 1320 but contains work of several different periods. It has a simple oak, carved altar, interesting stained glass and window surrounds and is unusual because the aisles are wider than the nave. According to local tradition, Columbus prayed here before setting out to discover the New World, together with a Galway sailor called Rice de Galvey who accompanied him on the voyage. In the church you can see the colours of the Connaught Rangers, who fought in Spain, the Crimea and the First World War, and were the first regiment in the British Army to sing the "Tipperary" song.

Immediately behind the church, in Market Street, is the world-famed Lynch Window, which is so well-known because of the story behind the inscription on the tablet it carries: "This ancient memorial of the stern and unbending justice of the chief magistrate of this city, James Lynch Fitzstephen, elected Mayor A.D. 1493, who condemned and executed his own guilty son, Walter, on this spot, has been restored to this, its ancient site, A.D. 1854, with the approval of the Town Commissioners . . ."

Walter Lynch Fitzstephen, a charming young man with athletic prowess, accordingly well-liked by the townspeople, was nineteen when his father returned from a trip to Spain, bringing with him the son of a Spanish friend, Gomez, who was to spend a year or two in Ireland. Gomez, almost the same age as Walter, was a quiet boy, but they quickly became friends and constant companions, even making a threesome with Agnes, the beautiful local girl with whom

Walter was in love. They were often seen together at social functions, and on one of these occasions Walter, thinking Gomez was receiving too much attention from Agnes, grew jealous. They quarrelled about this and Walter left the gathering feeling rather violent, a state of mind in which he continued the next night when, passing near Agnes' home, he saw a strange man leaving.

Impulsively, he followed the man, who grew frightened and ran towards a lonely and deserted part of town where Walter, crazed with jealousy, sank a small sword into his heart and threw him into the river. Too late, he had recognised the man as his friend Gomez whom he knew to be a regular visitor at Agnes's house because he was teaching her father Spanish. He was overcome by remorse, and waited until dawn, when he could report his guilt. This he did, before a big group of police and militia led by his father, the Mayor, who was also the magistrate with power of life and death. Distressed, he had his son put in prison near their home, and made preparations for a trial. Because the people thought so well of the boy, they joined with relatives in trying to dissuade the father from his duty.

Walter pleaded guilty and the death sentence was given, but the official executioner refused to carry it out. The crowd, clamouring for Walter's release, were suddenly hushed as the Mayor, determined that justice should be done, embraced and then hanged his son. Calling at first for the Mayor's death, the crowd faded away as the horror of his action struck them. The father died of grief, having given to the English language one of its ugliest words—lynching.

From the Lynch Window, you can work your way round to the Salmon Weir, from the bridge above which, in season, you will see hundreds of salmon on their way to the spawning beds in Lough Corrib. Many, along with the eels also found in the weir, end up just as I like them, on a table in the *Claddagh Grill* which I have already mentioned. It is worth noting that the Galway Fishery, when first described in historical records of 1283, was valued at $53, then a sizable amount, was sold to Edward Eyre for $720 in 1710, and after changing hands twice more, was bought by its present owners in 1954, for $192,000. Considering the quality and flavour of the fish, I reckon it was a fair price.

Alongside the Corrib river, just below the weir, a new Cathedral is being built, and also in this area is the University College. If you remain on that side of the river, you can continue to the site of the Claddagh, which is supposed to be the oldest fishing village in Ireland, but there is nothing to see, the old cottages having been replaced by modern houses. Beyond is the town's own seaside resort, Salthill (see below). Instead of going out this way, you can complete your main town tour by crossing over Wolfe Tone Bridge or O'Brien's Bridge—where houses are set unusually close to one of the weirs—and seeing the Spanish Arch. This is one of the few remaining parts of the big wall which enclosed the town in the twelfth century.

Where some of the stones have crumbled away at the top, an effigy of the Madonna and Child looks out, framed by the windswept overhang of a tree. At the side of the arch, and very much in contrast with its antiquity, is the sparkling house of the famous sculptress and writer, Mrs. Clare Sheridan, a cousin of Sir Winston Churchill. Long ago, the area in front of the archway was a fish market. Nearby, you can sit on the seats at the side of the fast-flowing Corrib, over the sound of which come the snapping cries of the constantly-wheeling seagulls. Or you can go down the Long Walk, where the Spanish grandees and their ladies used to promenade past the big sailing ships from Italy, Spain and France which once moored here to offload cargoes of wine and silk. At a certain time in summer, this is the place from which to watch the netting of salmon from a special floating platform in the middle of the river.

Galway has many good shops, where you can buy all the well-known Irish products such as linen, tweeds and Waterford glass, as well as things made of marble from nearby Connemara. Galway is itself noted for handwoven tweeds. I have referred to Stephen Faller, the jewellers. Apart from all the items you would expect to find there, they also sell the Claddagh rings and Tara brooches, gold and silver charms of the Galway Sword and Mace, the Ardagh Chalice, the Cross of Cong, and the Spanish Arch. Almost opposite is McCullagh's, a good bookshop also selling guides and maps—another with an enormous range of books is O'Gorman's in Shop Street. A secondhand bookshop and art gallery is Kenny's in High Street, where you can also obtain Connemara marble and Irish copper jewellery. Burke's sell fishing tackle. Facing is Dillon's, "the original" Claddagh Ring Shop, established in 1750.

Confectionery, sweet and paper shops are usually open until 11 at night, even in winter. At *Lydon's Restaurant* and delicatessen there is always a huge display of cakes and pastries. Many of the shops are modern, both in their content, and the way in which they present the goods, but I was amused to see one window displaying lawnmowers, guitars, china, carpets and motor-bicycles all together!

Apart from the famous Galway Races at the end of July or beginning of August, the National Curragh Championships are held here in June, and in May, usually on the last Tuesday of the month, the May Fair takes place. On this occasion, the cattle are swum out from the Aran Islands to the boats which bring them to Galway (see page 153). Most lively event is the annual Oyster Festival in September, which reached its tenth year in 1964. This begins on a

Friday evening, with the opening of the Festival Bar—a "driftwood" bar, draped with fishing nets—at the *Great Southern Hotel*, which is Festival headquarters.

On the Saturday morning, everyone goes to taste the first oysters of the season on Clarenbridge Pier, conveniently near Paddy Burke's pub on the main road from Shannon Airport. The Oyster Queen is then received on her arrival in the horse-drawn Claddagh Coach. She opens the Festival and the crowd of visitors moves to a field with a large marquee where not only oysters but all the best seafood is served. The food is eaten to the accompaniment of a free supply of Guinness—the brewers make this kind of gesture on various occasions, but there is a great deal they do for good causes behind the scenes, without securing any publicity for themselves.

Intake carries on until the middle of the afternoon and, in the early evening, there is a reception back at the hotel, before a gala dinner, with top-level entertainers from Dublin. When dinner is over, the floor is cleared for dancing. On the Sunday morning, from the respectable, after-the-night-before hour of 11.30, until lunchtime, Irish coffee is served, and there is no limit to the amount visitors may drink.

The events and entertainments of the Festival are variable, and the promoters are always trying new ideas. One of the Holland-America Line ships which regularly came into Galway in the 1964 season was held for 24 hours so that the company could invite Festival guests to a dinner on board. There was a firework display from the ship which, moored close to Salthill, also provided a spectacle for the local people, who are also considered, and are encouraged, on the main Festival night, to visit their pubs. Some of the pubs serve oysters and enable visitors to come in and meet the local people.

Cost of the ticket covering the whole programme is about $14. For the number of oysters you can eat—which is not at all restricted—plus the splendid spread of the cold buffet and the unlimited Guinness, the dinners and other features mentioned, this seems very reasonable, especially as no profit is made. In any case, it's a wonderful chance to try those lovely Galway Bay oysters, that Corrib salmon and eel, and the Carrageen Surprise on the dinner menu— Carrageen is a "delicately flavoured junket" made from Carrageen moss collected on the seashore.

Menus in Galway also list partridge, woodcock, duck and other products of the shooting season at the appropriate time. Fishing, of course, is among the major sports of the area. Galway Bay Anglers' Club arranges weekend trips on Galway Bay. The charge is $2.40 per person daily, and gear can be hired when booking. Contact Salthill Rentals, Forster Park, Salthill. There is also a water-skiing club at Salthill. You can hire motor boats for trips on Lough Corrib, and temporary membership of boat clubs is available to visitors. Rowing-boats can be hired, too.

West of Galway, along the bay shore, is Salthill, with a good, sandy beach, from which you can bathe safely. There is a swimming pool, too, on the promenade, but this is for women and children—the men's bathing place is at Blackrock, where the promenade ends, and it has diving boards. On the Barna road out of Galway, the Silver Strand is another good bathing place, and I have mentioned several more from Barna to Spiddal and beyond in the section dealing with Connemara.

Galway, of course, is an excellent base for tours around Connemara, Achill Island, the Cliffs of Moher, and many other places described in the following pages. If you are not using your own or a hired car, they can all be visited by coach. For further details, contact the C.I.E. office in Galway.

The most rewarding excursion that can be made from Galway—if you are in sympathy with things earthy and unspoiled—is a boat trip to the three Aran Islands which lie thirty miles from that port. In the steamer from Galway, the journey takes a little under three hours, calling at Inisheer and Inishmaan, the smaller islands—actually lying offshore while curraghs unload passengers and cargo—then going on to dock at Kilronan on Inishmore for a few hours in which visitors can see the island. Departure times and duration of the trip vary according to prevailing tides and weather—as C.I.E. operate the service, their office is again the best source of information on schedules.

Although there are guest houses and small cafés on Inishmore, the peace of the island is preserved, and there are many fine beaches. Of the numerous stone forts, Dun Aengus on Inishmore is the most impressive antiquity anywhere in Ireland. It perches at the edge of a cliff which rises sheerly from the sea three hundred feet below. It is thought that the other half of the semi-circular structure fell into the sea a long time ago. One authority has described Dun Aengus as "The most stupendous stone fort in Europe, perhaps the greatest military monument in the world, with walls eighteen to twenty feet thick, compared to some of which those of Mycene, the classic city of Agamemnon, are but insignificant". Also on Inishmore is Clochan na Carraige, a perfect ancient stone dwelling. At Killeany, in the southern part of the island, is Teampall Bheanain, thought to be the smallest church in the world— 10 feet 9 inches by 7 feet in area, although its height is 15 feet.

The character of the sturdy islanders was memorably portrayed not only by J. M. Synge in his *Riders to the Sea* and *The Aran Islands* but also in the film *Man of Aran*. Their livelihood has been secured only through extremely hard work, using sand and seaweed to create soil which would feed their livestock, and by fishing the surrounding waters from their curraghs (see below). They spin and weave their own clothes. Most of them wear the white bawneen coat, the many-coloured woollen crios belt, and the heel-less pampootie, a rough hide shoe.

Apart from the chance to meet these fine people, Aran offers good bathing, boating, fishing and scenery. It is a wonderful place for unusual "away-from-it-all" holidays, as well as an attractive excursion.

THE CURRAGH

The Aran islander's boat, the curragh, has a light framework of timber laths covered with tarred canvas. It is a variant of the coracle used in ancient times, which was made of wickerwork covered with animal skins. Centuries of experience had been handed down to the men who designed them, with the bow and stern rising clear above the water so that the craft can ride any kind of sea.

Lightness makes it very manageable, and a gentle pull on either oar is enough to turn it, but its lack of weight, and the fact that it has no keel, make it unsteady and dangerous in the hands of any unskilled person. Aran boatmen say that a man must keep his tongue in the centre of his mouth when he is in a curragh! Everything actually does depend on a perfect balance. Because of its frail construction, of course, the curragh can be damaged on rocky shores; a jagged rock or even a limpet will rip open the tarred canvas bottom, although damage is easily repaired.

Normally the curragh carries from two to four oarsmen, each pulling on a pair of oars, the three-man boat being most common. After use, the curragh is carried ashore and turned upside down at a position well clear of the high-water mark. Groups of the craft can be seen clustered around the coves of the islands, and it is interesting to note that while, for instance, as a Kerry farmer, you could borrow anything from your neighbour in the next field—where he could see you and signal if he wanted it back—you cannot borrow a man's curragh, as he may need it suddenly and urgently.

To the inhabitants of Inisheer and Inishmaan, the smaller islands, the curragh is even more important than it is to those on Inishmore, for only the latter has a quay, and the craft is used to convey all their merchandise to the others. The s.s. *Dun Aengus*, on which you may travel if you visit the islands, takes passengers, cargo and mail to Inishmore twice weekly, and stands off the smaller islands while the curraghs are rowed out to make collection.

Although the landing of ordinary goods on the islands has its problems, none are so great as on the occasions when the men of Aran, who are both fishermen and farmers, have to ship their cattle to the nearest fair, in Galway. With some difficulty, pigs and donkeys can be carried in curraghs, but bullocks and horses have to be towed to the steamer. On the day of a fair, animals to be shipped are gathered on the beach and guarded until the steamer is in sight. Then a halter is put round the neck of one animal which is led into the sea with people pushing it from behind, towards a curragh lying a few yards off-shore. A man leans over the stern, takes a firm grip of the halter, holding the animal's head above water while the other two men in the curragh row to the steamer as fast as they can go, the animal swimming gamely behind. The animal is hoisted on board the steamer with a sling and derrick, and the process is repeated until all the animals are aboard. The most difficult part of the operation is placing the sling under the animal's belly, a feat managed by the man in the stern of the curragh, holding the head with one hand and manoeuvring the sling into position with the other.

Many aspects of Aran island life depend on the curragh. On Inishmaan there is no priest. Every Sunday and holy day the curate of Inisheer crosses over to say Mass. Inisheer has no doctor, so when the nearest one, on Inishmore, three miles away, is needed, often at night, three neighbours of the sick person put on oilskins and go out in a curragh to fetch him, even during a gale. The craft is also one of the islanders' main sources of income. During the herring and mackerel seasons, the men spend their nights at sea, shooting and hauling their nets many times between sunset and dawn.

CONNEMARA

Connemara, the western part of County Galway, between Lough Corrib and the Atlantic, is a thinly-populated, wild and rugged area, although its wonderful scenic beauty is occasionally softened down in isolated spots. It can be seen in sections on half-day tours, or a whole-day tour can take in its highlights, and these tours can be made from several of the hotels in the region, or using Galway as a base. There are good places at which to stay in Bally-nahinch, Cashel, Roundstone, Clifden and Renvyle—which I will describe—but if you are staying in Galway, you can make one of them your target for lunch on a day-tour, and the time you start depends on which one you choose. Clifden is 49 miles from Galway.

Your itinerary can be varied in many ways, according to what you want to do, and how much time you have, and the management or hall porter of your hotel will help you with your planning. One of two routes I covered—this was an all-day run—began at Galway, driving through Moycullen, Oughterard and Maam Cross to Recess. Very surprisingly, this last place has had little publicity—despite the international fame of the Connemara green marble which comes from its quarries. These are owned by Michael Joyce, and you will see a sign leading you to his display of the many delightful souvenir pieces made from the marble—in several lovely variations of the colour—in a shop where handknit goods and coloured postcards of the area are on sale too. This is also the only place for miles at which you can buy a drink, a cup of tea or coffee—but no food is served, although you can buy groceries there if you happen to be camping or picnicking. It is worth noting that King George V visited these quarries, from which the marble—again surprisingly!—is exported to Italy, actually to an English sculptor there. Some goes to Germany. Supplies are also sent to a Torquay jeweller, who sets the marble in various pieces he sells, and to a Birmingham builder who makes bar-counters from the material. Famous buyers of table-tops from the Recess shop were Bing Crosby and Bob Hope.

After leaving Recess, ignore the first sign on your left to Cashel, and continue instead to *Ballynahinch Castle Hotel*, on the turning for Roundstone a little further on. If you are not staying in Galway, and Connemara is part of your all-Ireland tour, this is a place at which you are bound to stop if you can. I say if you can, because it is one of those hotels which are fully booked in season, mainly with fishermen who return year after year, and you need to make a reservation well in advance.

Against a background of the mountains known as the Twelve Bens, the hotel, on the southern shore of Ballynahinch Lake, was originally an O'Flaherty stronghold, then became the home of the Martins, the family whose story was told in the novel *The Martins of Cro Martin*, by Charles Lever. Its most famous member was Richard, called "Hair-Trigger Dick"—the name was earned at duelling with pistols—and later "Humanity Dick". Despite strong opposition, he founded the R.S.P.C.A.

The Martin family settled in Galway County about the fourteenth century, and the castle with its estate came into possession of Captain Richard Martin, a former officer in the army of James II, and grandfather of "Humanity Dick". The latter, born in 1754, was educated at Harrow and Trinity College, Cambridge. He was idolised by his father's tenants even as a schoolboy—they turned out to greet him when he came to Ballynahinch for holidays. Unlike the much-feared landlords of the period, the Martins were feudal lords who never evicted their tenants for non-payment of rent, and the tenants always remained loyal.

The relationship proved invaluable in later years when Dick Martin's fast living and lavish hospitality led him into very considerable debt. Sheriff's officers on their way to serve writs at the castle were always stopped by the vassal-tenants long before they reached it, and one was forced to eat the document he carried, after it had been soaked in native whiskey.

When Martin's Cruelty to Animals Act of 1822 was under debate in the House of Commons, an opponent of the Bill remarked on the inconsistency of his concern for dumb animals with his love of duelling, and Martin answered: "An ox cannot hold a pistol, sir." Four years later, he lost his seat, gave up his estate at the age of seventy-two and fled to France, leaving his son with debts worth a hundred thousand pounds. A great-grandson, by his second marriage to a niece of Henry Fielding, the novelist, was later a judge in the Court of Appeal of British Columbia.

After passing from the hands of the courts into those of

two successive private owners, the castle became the property in 1925 of the Maharaja Ranjitsinhji, the Indian prince and famous cricketer. Like Dick Martin, he too was made subject to numerous legends, most of them quite untrue. For instance, he was credited with having no less than a hundred wives because of whom he never had a moment's peace. In fact, he was a celibate. "Ranji", as the people of the district called him, employed much local labour, and there was only one occasion on which he learned what his employees thought of him. He was out fishing on the lake with an old gillie rowing his boat and, unexpectedly, hooked an enormous salmon. The gillie had never seen one so large and, anxious for it to be landed safely, began bawling instructions.

"Take him aisey, your worship! Keep up the top of the rod, your excellency! Let him run, your grace! Wind him up now again, your majesty! Not so hard, your Riverence." But his warning came too late. The rod sprang erect in Ranji's hands and the line wrapped itself around the gillie's head. With a strong pull on the oars, the gillie shot the boat towards the shore, with Ranji sprawled over the stern. Between his toothless gums, the old gillie contemptuously muttered "You b——, black b——! What could you know about playing a salmon?"

In his time, Ranjitsinhji spent $48,000 improving the property, with numerous jetties and piers as well as shelters around the waterside between the estuary at Toombeola past the Derryclare butts and as far as the wonderful Lough Inagh.

Anglers tend to take up most of the accommodation in the summer, but Ballynahinch Castle also looks after guests who want just a quiet holiday. Those who do will also find the best time to go there is April to May. The fishing season actually starts with the run of spring salmon in March,

157

and is well into its stride by early summer. The salmon weigh from five to thirty pounds, sometimes more. It has been said that this is the largest and richest salmon and sea trout fishery in Europe. Thackeray, more than a century ago, wrote "Oh you, who laboriously throw flies in English rivers . . . how would you rejoice to have but an hour's sport in Derryclare or Ballynahinch where you have but to cast, and lo! a big trout springs at your fly."

The hotel has a wonderful old fishing room where there is a bar, and in which catches are weighed, hung and photographed by the visiting fishermen. Non-angling guests will share their delight with the fine view from the terrace and some of the rooms of the Ballynahinch river curving away attractively, rather like a miniature—at least in shape—of the Thames at Richmond. Write to the management for the hotel tariff—incidentally, they do not permit you to take dogs or other pets there—or for the fishing rates. Accommodation for fishermen is also limited—not by the volume of fish, but by the facilities available—and advance booking is advisable for them, too.

Shooting on the hotel estate of 1,000 acres, and its rough shooting preserve of more than 30,000 acres, is grouse from the beginning of September to the end of October, and woodcock from November to February. The woodcock shooting is said to be first rate. There is also wild goose and pheasant shooting in the preserve. Dogs, of course, are allowed for guests who come to shoot, and kennels are available. The management will provide dogs if given advance notice, and, for those who do not know, recommend a setter as the best dog for grouse, a retriever for woodcock. Ask the hotel for further details and charges. Also bear in mind that gun Importation and Shooting Licences are needed. Both are obtainable from The Department of Justice, Upper Merrion Street, Dublin 2.

Another sport which visitors unexpectedly find possible to indulge in this area is pearl-fishing. The tiny rivers running down from the hills contain shellfish like mussels, bearing pearls which although mostly of poor quality and worth very little, are occasionally good enough specimens to realise about $24 apiece.

The famous Connemara pony has its home in the Ballynahinch district, and many can be seen wandering around half wild in the vicinity of the Castle. How they originated is not certain. One school says they were introduced to Connemara by the Martins. Another suggests they are descended from a cargo of Arab ponies which swam ashore from a wrecked ship of the Armada. They are easily trained and become excellent riding ponies for children. The best of them are paraded every August at the Connemara Pony Show and Sale which takes place at Clifden (see page 161).

On an artificial island in Ballynahinch lake is a "crannog" —a lake-dwelling of prehistoric origin and very well preserved. Also, in the north-west corner of the lake, is an old island fortress of the O'Flahertys, believed to have been built with stones looted from the abbey at Toombeola, the remains of which can be seen further down the river beyond Toombeola bridge. The fortress, used by the Martins, had two purposes, one credible—the manufacture of "poitheen", the native whiskey—the other questionable but probable, as a prison for people Humanity Dick found guilty of cruelty to animals.

Turning right from the driveway of Ballynahinch Castle, and following the road for the coast, you come to the little *Angler's Rest* inn and its annexe, the delightful little row of sparkling white cottages alongside. These were also the property of Ranjitsinhji. Owner of the inn is Mrs. Kathleen Prynne, a Londoner, and a major attraction she can offer is 4,000 acres of rough shooting. There is also good fishing.

Instead of going straight on to Roundstone, turn left to Cashel at the junction a little way beyond the inn. At Cashel you will find the Zetland, a visit to which is bound to be good for you because, with the fisheries in Gowla, Inver and Ballynahinch Upper Waters, it is owned by the British Guinness Company. It stands in a superb position on a most unusually-contoured bay in which, at high tide, everything jutting out of the waters becomes hidden below the surface—except the biggest promontory, at the right, which is transformed into an island. If you want a quiet holiday, here is another place where you can sit and admire the view, which, in the foreground, includes the garden fondly tended by Manager Michael Freyer's wife. The best time is from the end of October to June. In fact it is the only time to be sure of what you want, as the hotel is fully booked in July, August and September every year, by fishermen who keep returning. Write to the hotel as early as possible—you might find a vacancy just when you want it.

The peak of the salmon and sea trout season here is from the beginning of July to 12th October. In the spring, brown trout fishing is free, and hotel guests can fish Clifden Trout Anglers' water. Any licences required are obtainable at the hotel, which also provides gillies and boats on all the lakes. There is rough shooting in 10,000 acres of bog, lake and estuary. This is free, apart from the services of gillies, which are charged at the same rate as for fishing. Incidentally, the hotel serves only *table d'hôte* meals, has no *à la carte* menu. The restaurant and the comfortable lounges are very attractive.

Sheep, cows and donkeys constantly stray on to the road all over Ireland, and I met a great many on my way to

16. Shark fishing in Keem Bay, Achill Island

17. Benbulben, Co. Sligo

18. Lough Gill, Co. Sligo

19. Marble Hill Beach, Dunfanagh, Co. Donegal

Roundstone, a little coastal village in a district of considerable interest to naturalists. At the roadside, too, I saw the locals hanging seaweed out to dry. As you come into Roundstone, the *Seal's Rock Hotel* is on your right. A short distance beyond the village is a fine sheltered beach, and another is about five miles before Clifden. Good beaches are found at several places in this area. Just before Clifden, there are signs to the memorial for Alcock and Brown—half a mile in one direction—and 1½ miles in another, to the place where they landed at the end of the memorable first transatlantic flight in June, 1919.

Clifden town of itself is not very distinctive, but it has an attractive setting on the edge of the Atlantic and against a mountain background, and there is much to see and do in the area. The Connemara Pony Show is held here in August, together with an exhibition of native arts and crafts. Flat race meetings are also held at Clifden and other nearby places. There are safe beaches for swimming, many walking and mountain climbing opportunities, fresh water angling and shooting (wild geese, duck and several kinds of plover). On one of the walks, you can see the ruins of Doon Castle, an O'Flaherty stronghold in Queen Elizabeth I's time.

Both Clifden Bay and Cleggan, a small fishing port seven miles away, offer good sea fishing. From Cleggan, you can reach Inisbofin and other neighbouring islands. Near the Alcock and Brown landing place is the ruined Marconi Wireless Station which was opened in October, 1907, provided the first transatlantic radio service and was extremely important in the First World War. It was powered by turf from the surrounding bog. The airship R34, on its transatlantic flight in 1919, also stopped at Clifden. Four miles away is the only coral beach in Europe, where you can find many interesting shells. Stay at the

Clifden Bay Hotel, a spacious and comfortable place with food supplied from its own farm.

North-west, at the end of the road from Letterfrack, is Renvyle, where the hotel of the same name has a very good reputation, and there is some of the finest coastal scenery in the area. From Letterfrack, and particularly between Kylemore and Leenane, it is very impressive. Above the three Kylemore lakes is the majestic castellated Kylemore Abbey, where Irish Benedictine nuns run a girls' boarding school. As the Abbey brochure says, nearly all Irish place-names are descriptive as well as musical, also a link with the past—good reasons why successive generations do not readily part with them. The original owners of Kylemore Castle gave it this name, derived from the Irish for "big wood". How they acquired the property makes a story with some fairy-tale characteristics—at least for the lady concerned.

Mitchell Henry, a Manchester surgeon and financier, who also owned Stratheden House in London, had just married the lovely Margaret Vaughan of County Down in the north. On their honeymoon, they came to Connemara from Galway, and picknicked at the side of the road near Kylemore Pass. Margaret was delighted with the setting and expressed a wish to live at the hunting lodge which was the only building in view. The Mitchell Henrys became the owners of the lodge and with it 9,000 acres of moorland, lake and mountain. Mitchell became M.P. for County Galway, and the happy couple began planning Kylemore Castle, which cost $3 million and took seven years to build. The whole fascinating story is told in a booklet written by one of the nuns and which is on sale at the Abbey.

I said the acquisition of the property and creation of the castle was a fairy story, but of course, it was facilitated by Mitchell Henry's great wealth, and the story ended very

162

tragically for him, as the booklet also tells. Margaret contracted Nile fever in Cairo and died there while on holiday. Their daughter was killed near home when the pony pulling her trap was frightened and threw her from a bridge on to the rocks below. Then Mitchell lost his millions with the collapse of his investments in gold and diamond mines and other stocks. Finally he lost a lawsuit and in consequence, his London home.

The castle was sold, for a fraction of what he had spent on it, to an English duke who spent a considerable sum making tasteless changes, and ultimately mortgaged the property to a moneylender. After the Anglo-Irish War, it became the home of the nuns of St. Benedict. Their fine story is also contained in the booklet, underlining the loss of their Abbey at Ypres in the First World War, and dealing with their return to Ireland. The publication is full of interest, and well worth reading if you can obtain a copy. It is only fair to mention that although, at the time of writing, visitors were allowed by arrangement with the Tourist Board, you should check with their offices whether this is still in force. Even if it is not, you can see the great building from the road nearby, and in any case, try to find the booklet.

From Kylemore, as I have already said, the scenery on the drive to Leenane is magnificent. There is one really outstanding view of Killary Harbour, with the mountains receding behind each other on either side. The harbour, which has provided anchorage for the Royal Yacht, runs inland for some ten miles.

When you reach Leenane, come down to Maam. At this point, you can either go through Maam Cross and drive on to Galway through Screeb Lodge and the lovely coast road round to Spiddal and Barna; via Maam Cross and Oughterard; or, on the north side of Lough Corrib via

Cornamona, Cong and Headford. If you are not staying in Galway and your tour continues north, this last route is the best, cutting out Headford and continuing north from Cong. Having done all three, I can tell you that the coastal run is in many ways the best, although the stretch between Maam Cross and Oughterard is captivatingly wild, and the country around Cong is pleasant. Between Maam and Cong, too, on the lakeside road, mountains provide the background, and there are fast running streams and falls—the streams disappear under the road and come out at the other side. They are near and clear, and you pass peat seams giving out fine rich chocolate brown pieces ready to be dried for burning. The whole area has a rugged beauty, highlit, too by the heathers and the white cottages and groups of sheep dotted everywhere. There are crags near Inveran, around which there was, at the time of my visit, a rather bumpy stretch of road, which improves just before Spiddal, where you will come across dark, blue-washed cottages looking most attractive with the white sea-rollers on the unspoiled coastline beyond. From Spiddal to Barna, the coast road is very good and there is a pleasant site for caravans behind the garage on the shore.

Connemara is certainly one of the most beautiful areas in the country, and its scope is inexhaustible, offering as it does something to interest every kind of holidaymaker. Scenically, the region is dominated by the Twelve Bens, part of the Beanna Beola range. The Bens cover an area of 42 square miles, and range in height from 1,700 to 2,400 feet.

Geological students have found many different mineral deposits in the area. Forty years ago, there were silver mines at Maam, and silver, copper and lead still exist in the district. Local talk periodically suggests that there is gold in the hills, too.

Of course, the Connemara mountains attract an increasing

number of climbers, both the experienced ones who can scale the heights of the Bens, and the less energetic visitor who aspires to more reasonable levels. The ascent of Errisbeg, a few miles west of Ballynahinch, is particularly recommended. From its 987 feet summit, you are able to see at least three hundred lakes, many with islets, and all teeming with brown trout. Have fun counting them—the lakes, not the trout.

CONG

Through Cornamona, you come to Cong. Its name means "neck of land" and is derived from its position on the narrow strip which separates Lough Corrib and Lough Mask. The surrounding area is thickly wooded, and the place is very much a shooting and fishing centre. In England it is well-known largely because of Ashford Castle, which was built by the late Lord Ardilaun, took thirty years to complete, at a cost of more than $2.4 million, and became a hotel in 1939. It is famed for its comfort and food, and is self-contained with its own farm, dairy, fishery and salmon smoking plant. There is a gift shop and a cinema in the hotel, facilities for billiards and table tennis. Dancing takes place occasionally. When you drive in across its wonderful cut stone bridge, in effect, you are cutting yourself off for a while to enjoy the peace and quiet intentionally available here, in sumptuous surroundings.

In the Corrib Aperitif Lounge, probably the most splendid room in the castle, the sides of the service counter are decorated with bird and animal carvings, over 200 years old, and on the fireplace—of carved oak inlaid with ebonite—is a figurehead of King Roderick O'Connor, last of the native monarchs to be High King of All Ireland. The finest feature in the castle is the huge oak inglenook and fireplace in the reception room, which rises more than twenty feet to the ceiling. There are 300 acres of grounds, with many lakeside and riverside walks, caves to explore, croquet and putting lawns, a swimming pool, boating and tennis.

Lough Corrib, second largest lake in Ireland, offers what many consider to be the best all-round free fishing in the world! This includes salmon, trout, bream, rudd, pike and perch. Experts also say that Lough Mask has the best wet and dry fly brown trout fishing in Ireland. Fishing is free on both lakes, apart from the boatman's services and meals. Powered boats are available, and the castle has a fully-stocked fishing tackle shop. The Dower House of the castle is the *Lisloughry Bay House Hotel*, two minutes drive away and under the same management. There are more than a hundred islands on Lough Corrib. Among them is Inchagoill, five miles by water from Cong, and on which is the Lugnaedon, one of the most ancient inscribed stones of the Christian period in the country. Captain Boycott, who gave his name to the English language, lived in Lough Mask House.

Inishmaine, five miles north of Cong, now connected with the mainland, was once an island on Lough Mask, and there are some interesting ruins here. Other places to visit around Cong are the ruins of the Augustinian Abbey and nearby, the Monks' Fishing House. The latter has a trap-passage through which the water flowed and the story goes that when a fish entered the trap, it activated a cord to ring a bell in the kitchen, and gave indication of the supplies thus kept fresh until they were needed.

It took hundreds of men more than four years to work on the cutting for the canal which was built a hundred years ago to link the waters of the two lakes. The work included five locks, and after completion it was discovered that the

166

water only soaked through the porous limestone. Since that time, apart from a small section at the Lough Mask end, the canal has not held any water. The two lakes are connected by subterranean channels with a great many caverns, through which the water can be seen flowing at some distance below. Some of these can be entered and followed —especially the impressive "Pigeon Hole"—but it is advisable to explore them with the help of a guide. On several sites around the castle, there are "crusheens"—little crosses of wood. Every time a funeral passes into Cong, friends and relatives of the deceased follow an ancient custom in making a small cross, or raising the pile of stones on which one of them rests. Incidentally, the famous Processional Cross of Cong, a very fine piece of metalwork, is now in the National Museum, Dublin.

Around the plain of Southern Moytura, between Cong and the Neale, is a strange collection of stone monuments and man-made caves. Traditionally, it is believed that this was the site of the first great battle fought between the Tuatha De Danann and the Firbolgs, about 400 B.C.

If you are returning southward after visiting Cong, it is worth stopping or calling at the whitewashed *Godefroys Hotel* in Greenfield, on the eastern edge of Lake Corrib, west of Headford. Here, apart from good food and comfort in a very peaceful position you will find you can hire a boat to go to Inchagoill Island. Nearby is the ruined Franciscan Abbey of Ross, the remains of the Church of St. Fursa, and those of Ballycurran Castle. There is also the ancient Templepatrick Church. The view from Greenfield takes in Inchiquin Island, Oughterard, the Connemara Mountains and the Joyce country. The hotel is on the water's edge.

After leaving Cong, head out northward to Partry. On the left, as you enter, you will see a small church, with a

headstone on the grave of Father James Corbett, a former
parish priest. His nephew, "Gentleman Jim" Corbett,
the famous world boxing champion, once visited the church
and donated two gateposts and a stained glass window.
Some time after he had gone, his uncle discovered that the
woman who had accompanied him was not his wife.
Because of this—so the story goes—Father James had the
window and gateposts removed.

BALLINTUBBER—THE ABBEY THAT REFUSED TO DIE

I drove on through Partry to meet Father Thomas A.
Egan, a much more enlightened priest of today. He has
things removed from his church, too—whatever replaces
them is part of a very careful plan for restoration. For he is
curate of a rather special church, Ballintubber Abbey. In
his beautifully-written booklet he gives the history of what
he calls "The Abbey That Refused to Die."

Built in 1216 by Cathal O'Conor, King of Connacht,
the Abbey is contemporary with the cathedrals of Notre
Dame and Chartres, and is older than Westminster Abbey.
The original foundation of the latter was made by Edward
the Confessor in 1065, and demolished later to make way
for the present building which dates from 1245. Ballintubber goes back even further than 1216, standing as it does
on the site where a church was founded by St. Patrick in 441.
The meaning of the Irish name for Ballintubber is "home-
stead of the well of St. Patrick". So for 1,500 years, there
has been a Christian church in this place.

Mass has been celebrated in the Abbey without a break
for more than 700 years—on the original thirteenth-century
altar still in use. In fact, apart from the timber roof dating
from 1889, and the stonework of the windows inserted in
the nave in 1846, the part of the abbey still used is entirely
unchanged since 1216.

What was the mortuary chapel, now the sacristy, contains the tomb of Theobald of the Ships—the first Viscount Mayo, and son of Grace O'Malley, the famous sea-queen. He was murdered outside the Abbey in 1629. Part of the elaborate carvings on the base of the tomb were badly mutilated by Cromwell's soldiers in 1653, the year when they destroyed most abbey buildings. Although the external roof was lost, the internal stone-vaulted roof of the chancel and the old sacristy and side-chapels were preserved intact. It was this that led to its use and the long unbroken record of years in which the Mass was offered there. American visitors are always awed by the fact that Columbus discovered their country 300 years after the abbey was founded.

It stands in a hollow, close to Lake Carra, which has receded since the abbey was built at the water's edge. Many churches and monasteries were set in similar positions, ensuring adequate water supplies and plenty of good fishing. About twenty years ago, the hulk of a primitive boat used in those times was dug out of the land around the abbey. Among the many notable features of the interior, I was very fascinated with the wonderful pigmentation and texture in some of the walls, especially the one from which a door leads to the sacristy. There are some stained-glass windows which, although contemporary, are well-blended into the building. This is an example of the careful planning in the restoration work, as I saw also from the numbered stones laid out behind the abbey. The local people, both Protestant and Catholic, take a great interest in the work, and much land in the area has been donated free in order to facilitate further excavation.

Father Egan, to whom I am indebted for permission to include in the above description facts from his booklet, hopes that funds will become available to complete restoration in time for the 750th anniversary of the foundation in

1966, when a special commemorative stamp will be issued. I recommend you to get a copy of the booklet, which is well-distributed in the country as well as being on sale at the abbey. Being the first work of its kind on the abbey, it has been very much in demand by various authorities, writers and students. During the very extensive research he carried out while preparing the booklet, Father Egan on one occasion spent many hours in a certain library, only to find a little while afterwards that he had mislaid his notes. Upsetting though this was, he went back and carried out his search all over again, this time working his way through with greater ease, and was rewarded when he uncovered additional material unnoticed during the first attempt.

There is no charge for admission to the abbey. In the graveyard alongside, under the big ash tree, is the grave of Sean na Sagart—John the Priest-Hunter, who earned a Judas wage for every priest he betrayed; and almost opposite the abbey is a lovely contemporary statue of the Madonna and Child, set in a wayside shrine.

Ballintubber was dispossessed by Henry VIII, partly destroyed by the Cromwellians, twice burned. Restoration was carried out at intervals. The abbey was never completely abandoned. Divine service always continued to be held there. Father Egan and everyone concerned, in past and present, are rightly proud of "The Abbey That Refused to Die".

CROAGH PATRICK

West of Ballintubber, and near Westport, is Croagh Patrick, Ireland's Holy Mountain, to which the annual pilgrimage is second in importance to, and in many ways more impressive than, the one made to Lough Derg (see page 181). Every year, some 80,000 people, many of them

170

barefoot, make the ascent of the mountain (2,510 feet). For more than 1,500 years, pilgrims have followed the example of St. Patrick who, in 441, spent the forty days of Lent praying and fasting at the summit. Although the first part of the climb is fairly easy, the second part, over rough, stony ground, is a much greater test of endurance. In ancient times, a road extended from Ballintubber to the mountain.

At Knock, east of Ballintubber, the parish church, once the scene of an apparition of the Blessed Virgin, is another place of regular pilgrimage.

ACHILL ISLAND

Continuing what I hope will be your leisurely tour of the country, you now have the choice of heading north to Sligo and the nearby resorts, or diverting through Westport to see the wild and unspoiled Achill Island, where the neat, white houses stand out in contrast with the terrain.

Your way to Achill lies through Westport although, if you are coming from Ballintubber Abbey, you need not go back along the road south to Westport. Returning from the Abbey to the Galway–Castlebar road, cross over towards Killavala, so that you quickly reach the road to Westport.

It is quite a pleasant little town. During the season, you will be able to visit Westport House, home of the Marquess of Sligo. This is situated one mile from the town, and although you pay for admission, there are no guided tours—you can walk round quite freely. Reductions are made for parties, a free car park is provided, and teas are served.

On the site of the house, which is of the Georgian period, the ancient castle of the O'Malleys stood, and the dungeons

171

can still be seen. The position gives fine views over Clew Bay and the Atlantic, of Achill and Clare islands, and of Croagh Patrick. The original house was built by ancestors of the present Marquess, Colonel John Browne and his wife—she was a great-great-granddaughter of Grace O'Malley. There was no lake or dam, and the water lapped the walls. In 1730, the east front was built—as it is now—of the best limestone from the quarry near the farmyard, and by local craftsmen. The house was finally completed by the English architect James Wyatt, who also laid out Westport town. Among the contents of the rooms on show there is a collection of old English and Irish silver. The paintings include a portrait of the second Marquess, who spent four months in an English gaol for bribing British seamen in time of war to bring his ship, full of antiquities, from Greece to Westport.

Hotels in the area include *Newport House* at Newport and *Breaffy House* at Castlebar. Going on to Newport and Mulranny, there is some interesting countryside, and at Mulranny, close to the road, is another of the Great Southern hotels.

Beyond here, the terrain becomes rather wild, and you will enjoy many glimpses of the sea and rocky headlands. Achill is no longer an island. A bridge now connects it with the mainland, and when you have driven over, I recommend you to make for Keel and settle in at the *Amethyst Hotel*. Owner Mrs. Thea Boyd says she doesn't feel that the twenty-nine years she has been there is a long time, but I suppose that anyone living in a place which faces as it does the dramatic Minaun Cliffs towering over the lovely Keel Strand would soon lose all sense of time. Anyhow, I suggest you try it and see.

The *Amethyst* has plenty of atmosphere, centred mainly round the big raftered dining-room, with its peat fire burning cosily at one end where some very relaxing armchairs are placed. Somehow, I was reminded of places we used to see in the kind of films no longer made, or described in the kind of books no longer written. Like those, the *Amethyst* has warmth, homeliness and friendliness. As in the books and films, you often hear the whine of the Atlantic wind but here it doesn't induce a spooky feeling. Instead, when it occurs, you have a peaceful inclination to huddle up gratefully by the fire. When I arrived on a rather blowy afternoon, I was greeted with tea and spice biscuits—sort of cookies with a plus—and by Rufus, the friendly ginger cat, quick to recognise a worshipper of felines rather than canines. Mrs. Boyd was not sure whether Rufus would still be around, old as he is, but you may be lucky. Yes, I strongly recommend you to let the *Amethyst* shine on you. And if you don't notice the fact for yourself, Mrs. Boyd will point out that amethyst is the prevailing colour in the mountains and the sky over Achill.

The beach, three miles long, a nine-hole golf course, and Keel Lake, holding numerous small brown trout and some sea trout, are all close to the hotel, which has a bar in its annexe. There is safe bathing, surf riding, plenty of scope for walking and climbing, seal caves to explore, sea trips to be made in curraghs or motor-vessels, and horses to be hired. Other good hotels on the island are the *Achill Head*, the *Wave Crest* and the *Atlantic*.

"The Deserted Village" ruins hug the lower slopes on the left flank of the big Slievemore Mountain (2,204 feet) and appropriately, it seems, there is a little cemetery with white gravestones alongside. These, in fact, are very recent. On the south slope of the mountain there are megalithic tombs, and on the island coast many promontory forts. Antiquities also include the Penal Altar at Keem Bay, the Sandhill Settlements on Keel Strand, fifteenth-century Kildownet Castle, once used by sea-queen Grace O'Malley,

173

and Bunowna booley-village. This last is derived from the Irish name for a milking place or summer hill dwelling, and you can see the huts once occupied during the summer when families and cattle migrated to the mountain pastures. The people of Dooagh "went to booly" near Slievemore, also at Annagh, and those from Slievemore came to Dooagh and Keel, as a result of which both villages were established as they are now. The practice has almost ceased, but it still takes place in France, Spain and Switzerland.

At the edge of the cliff, on the eastern end of Dugort Strand, is a children's burial ground, marked by a number of uninscribed slabs, and known locally as Cillin na Leanbh. Here on an open site, unbaptised children are buried. The custom of burying them in such sites instead of a normal graveyard used to be followed all over the country, but is now almost extinct. It is still practised on Achill. Sites chosen were usually in grass triangles formed by the crossing of three roads, then called Croisin na Leanbh, which name is still used on crossroads all over the country for that reason.

Walking around the bog-land, you will often see small huts, some with smoke pouring from their open doors. Inside these manure huts, a turf fire is lit to smoke the roof which is made of "scraws" cut from the bog and, after harvest, sometimes overlaid with rye-reed thatch. The roof is pulled off in the spring, broken up and used, with sea-weed, as manure for potatoes.

Spinning goes on in most of the island cottages, although this is dying out. The wool produced there—mostly on hand-operated wheels, although some have treadles—goes to a factory in Galway. Most houses make their own baskets. Lobster pots are also made, and the traditional curragh boats, of light planking on wooden ribs covered with tarred canvas. Although most men build their own

174

curraghs, this is steadily becoming a trade reserved to a few specialists in each village.

There are several tours to occupy your time while on Achill. On the road westward from Keel, through Dooagh, is Keem Bay. The road takes a steep rise at the side of the Croaghaun mountain, to the point where the bay can be seen far below. Along here the name Amethyst crops up again—for the quarry which is situated on both sides of the road. The trip is five miles, the last two of which are on poor, unsurfaced road—at the time of writing. If it is still in this condition when you go there, it is worth parking the car, and walking the final stretch. The whole tour can be done on foot.

The local people will persuade you that you must not miss the Atlantic Drive, beginning on the Cloghmore road leading south, from a point west of Achill Sound. Keep left at the fork past Kildownet Church and Castle, to Cloghmore. There you will see Achill Beg Island across the narrow channel. Bear west and follow the coast road for a few miles, a journey on which you will be glad you saw the fine views. Then make a sharp left turn at Ashleam village, continuing to Dooega and turning right after 2½ miles to come on to the main Achill Sound-Dooagh road.

From Bull's Mouth, in the north-eastern part of the island, you can call a boat ferry to take you to Inishbiggle Island; and another tour covers a circuit of the Curraun Peninsula, starting at Curraun, then going via Mulranny and Belfarsad. If Achill is your base for a lengthy stay, you can tour part of Connemara from there, or visit Pontoon on Lough Conn, which is the place to which I will now bring you. Achill is one of the places which remain vivid in my memory. Lough Conn is another. On a sunny morning, leaving Achill, I saw a column of filmy white mist rising from a calm sea, in front of Minaun. It was lit by the sun, and as I watched, it gradually disappeared.

PONTOON AND LOUGH CONN

There are two ways of reaching Pontoon. One road leads to the left as you approach Newport from Achill. The other starts at a left-hand turn on to the Castlebar road—opposite a set of pumps in Newport. This is the better one—a very pleasant run through hilly country. A little way along the route there is an attractive lake setting to the right, soon after you leave the mountains on your left.

Although Pontoon, on the peninsula where Lough Conn joins Lough Cullin, is called by that name, the postal address of the two hotels there is Foxford, Co. Mayo. The *Pontoon Bridge Hotel*, where Denis Murphy is the charming young manager, is on my list of special favourites. Incidentally, it has the same owner as *Tresanton Hotel* at St. Mawes in Cornwall. This is one of those places which has been modernised with taste, resulting in brightly decorated and furnished rooms—schemes that take away nothing of the homely warmth in an atmosphere where you can have a very peaceful holiday. Lounges, bar and bedrooms are all most comfortable.

A much more modest, but cheerfully managed and staffed place is *Healy's Anglers' Hotel*, on the curve of Lough Cullin as you approach. At whichever you stay, you will find free salmon, white and brown trout and pike fishing on both lakes, as well as smaller lakes nearby. Licences are required for salmon and sea trout. They cost $7.20 per season or $2.40 for seven days and in the case of *Pontoon Bridge Hotel*, they are available on the premises. The hotel also carries a big stock of tackle, and will obtain anything necessary within 24 hours. Both hotels will arrange for boats and gillies.

176

April and May are best for spring salmon here. Other seasons are: April, July and September for brown trout; July and October for sea trout; September and October for autumn salmon; June and September for grilse; August and November for pike. There are also about 5,000 acres of rough shooting in the area—but the going is hard, suitable only for the real enthusiast.

Immediately before *Healy's*, on the main road, a signpost indicates the road for the two-mile run to the Terrybaun Pottery at Bofeenaun, where lovely hand-made ware can be bought. It is the work of Grattan and Madeleine Freyer and their little staff. Mr. Freyer is the brother of Michael Freyer of the *Zetland Hotel* in Cashel. Among the things you can buy are terra cotta ware, slipware dishes, mugs and beakers, flower vases and bowls, candlesticks and lamp bases, coffee and breakfast sets.

Coming away from Pontoon, taking the left-hand fork in the direction of Ballina, Lough Conn got me, as so many lakes do. I think it is a very impressive stretch of water, with Nephin Mountain towering behind. It was slightly ruffled the day I was there, not wild, just talking a little, trying to say something to me. As usual, I answered back. I shall go back, too.

SLIGO

It would be a great mistake to rush through Sligo. There is more in this county than most people remember. Discover first, by slowing down on your way beyond Ballina, the pleasant little resort of Enniscrone; then a fine beach at Strandhill, 5½ miles west of Sligo, which has another of the Great Southern hotels; Benbulben Mountain looming at you as you curve around more beaches and bays in the

Yeats Country, notable also for lovely Lough Gill just south-east of the town.

Enniscrone has a good three-mile sandy beach curving round Killala Bay—one of those spots where one seems to need no more than time to watch the white-foamed waves coming in, shaped to the sweep of the bay. Overlooking it is the *Alpine Hotel*, and, ten minutes' walk away, a nine-hole golf course. You are on the beach in two minutes.

Above the long Strandhill beach is a funny old cannon without an identity plate. No one was abroad when I looked around there. Sorting out its history would make a holiday task for bright boys. Several small hotels here include the *Baymount*. But the beach does not always provide safe bathing, and it certainly is unsuitable for children.

Although there is a road round Lough Gill, it is easier to explore by boat, available at the riverside in Sligo. This way you will have a good view of the little Isle of Inishfree—the subject of Yeats' famous poem.

In Sligo itself, apart from the well-preserved ruins of the Abbey, and the little museum, you will find one building of much interest. This is the Cathedral, a Norman-style limestone building which although comparatively modern (1870) has a rather striking interior. The two-tone grey stonework has a very clean effect, and the slim, criss-crossed architraves, edged with gold paint, are fairly unusual. Big squat columns support a wide-arched gallery and a tier of curved windows meeting the gently vaulted roof from both sides of the central nave. Above the impressive heavy gold altar canopy, there are bold-coloured stained glass windows. There is an unusual feeling of spaciousness around the altar. In the aisles, the Stations of the Cross, in relief models, are carefully framed.

I advised you not to rush through this area. Much as he

loved it, Yeats put it rather differently, in the words you can see on his gravestone in the little churchyard at Drumcliff:

> "Cast a cold Eye
> On Life, on Death.
> Horseman, pass by."

Whatever your horse-power, you can go first to Rosses Point after leaving Sligo. It is a most pleasant little resort, mainly a golfing centre, but there is also good trout fishing. I liked the *Yeats Country Hotel* here, with its several lounges and light, airy restaurant. Of interest to literary visitors is the hotel collection of Yeats' early editions. Below is a deep, quite well-sheltered beach, and in the bay on the opposite side of the approach road, the huge figure of a mariner looks out to sea from a rounded plinth. There is a car park close to the beach.

A little way back on the road to Rosses Point, you can turn left on to the Bundoran road without returning to Sligo, and you see the sign pointing to the poet's grave. A little further west, still in country Yeats loved so well, is Lissadell. If you come back and turn left at Lissadell Church when you have been there, and then take the second road to the right—the signposting is limited around here—you will come to Grange, back on the Bundoran road, and from where you will have tantalising glimpses of the coastal scenery. These are effectively climaxed at the point where you turn left for Mullaghmore, to see a huge mansion rising from a mound with a small wood at its foot and a much larger one in the foreground. This belongs to Earl Mountbatten, and when not in residence, I gathered that he loans it to the Jesuits. Mullaghmore has a lovely sandy beach, a couple of small hotels on which I cannot comment as they were closed at the time of my visit, and yacht and boat builder Rodney Lomax, who hires out sailing dinghies for 35 c. an hour.

Before leaving Sligo County, two other things should be mentioned. The Yeats Society in Sligo town holds the Yeats International Summer School every August when, in addition to lectures and studies, visits are arranged to the various points of interest in the Yeats Country. Full details can be obtained from The Secretary, Yeats International Summer School, Stephen Street, Sligo (Tel.: Sligo 2680). Also worth noting is that the county is very rich in prehistoric monuments, a useful leaflet about which is obtainable from the Sligo Tourist Development Association. Nearly a score of items are listed.

So, leaving the haunting shadow of Benbulben and the words of the great poet behind us, as the travelogues used to say, we move on to the road for Donegal, heading towards Bundoran.

DONEGAL

Passing briefly into County Leitrim after leaving Mullaghmore, you come to Bundoran in Donegal, before which is Tullaghan, where the *Tullaghan Bay Hotel* is recommended. Bundoran is a developed resort neither too big nor too small, and spoiled only by the garish fun-fair on the beach road, which leads to another of the Great Southern hotels. This one is quite large and rambling, but seems friendly, and is set in its own grounds away from the other buildings near the beach. Bundoran is well-kept, has a certain sparkle of its own, and has an angling festival every year. A few miles further up the coast, you come to Rossnowlagh, which also has a good beach and at least one good hotel, the *Sand House*.

On a tour, you may prefer to do as I did after leaving Bundoran, and cross temporarily into Northern Ireland through Belleek, to see the famous pottery there, and the beautiful Loughs Erne and Macnean, with Enniskillen as a base. If so, stay at the *Imperial* in Enniskillen, where a steady conversion programme has created a very good house, in which the food, too, is excellent. Whether or not you make this diversion, you can visit Rossnowlagh before or afterwards. Actually, it is best to go there from Bundoran if you are diverting, to avoid doubling back the next day on the way out. I have dealt with the two Loughs, and County Fermanagh generally, in the section on Northern Ireland.

Another worthwhile diversion, which in this case is out of your way if you are already heading for Donegal town, but which is easy to make if you recross the border at Pettigo after leaving County Fermanagh, is the short run to Lough Derg. This is notable for Station Island, or St. Patrick's Purgatory. The tradition of the Saint's association with the island goes back 1,500 years, and makes it the country's most important place of pilgrimage. Rabelais and many others have written of the Purgatory, and it is said to have inspired Dante's *Divine Comedy*. The island is the most prominently marked feature of many sixteenth- and seventeenth-century maps. In the Middle Ages, most of the pilgrims were foreigners, and a list of visitors is still seen there. Even under oppression, pilgrimage continued, as it does today, between June and mid-August. Penitence of the most rigorous kind inspires this pilgrimage—three days of fasting, barefoot. Pilgrims can travel independently to the island during the season, and the railway company issues special tickets covering rail and bus journey to the lakeshore, from which there is a regular boat service to the island during season. Any enquiries can be addressed to the Rev. Prior, Lough Derg, Pettigo, Co. Donegal.

Two excellent little hotels in Donegal town are the *Central* and the *National*. Eat at either on your way north, or a little further on, at Joe Jackson's hotel in Ballybofee. The approach to Donegal town is through desolate terrain, but the journey is a short one, and most of the county is very attractive, especially on its coast. You will find sandy beaches at Mountcharles; the little village of Inver is noted for its sea and freshwater angling. Carrick is another good angling centre. There is a beach at Malinmore. Killybegs, Kilcar, Ardara, Rosbeg and Glenties are other places of interest in this part of Donegal, and among those where the famous tweeds and other products of the county are made. Narin has a fine strand and a nine-hole golf course.

From Glenties, you should drive northward through Maas, by Gweebarra Bay, The Rosses and Bloody Foreland until you see Inisbofin Island and beyond, the grim mass of Tory Island (see page 194). Facing Inishbofin, leading out from the tiny grass peninsula by the pier, is one of my favourite Irish strands, Magheroarty, a beautiful curving beach offering plenty of seclusion, and from which, when the tide is out, you can walk across to Inishbofin. Beyond the main sweep, out of sight, the beach extends further.

Continuing along the road for about seven minutes, you reach Gortahork, of no interest in itself, but most notable for *McFadden's Hotel*, run by Lillis and Bernie O'Leary, a charming couple who had admirably transformed half their house when I was there and told me most of the rest would be done by the time you read this book. A thoughtful contemporary architect has been employed by the O'Learys, as you can tell from such interesting details as the stone fireplaces in lounge and bar. The food here is very good.

Beyond Gortahork is Falcarragh where, if you stay at *McFadden's*, you will find another fine, long beach. The O'Learys told me that if visitors consult them each day they will advise on whether the wind is right either for Falcarragh or Magheroarty. You will always be able to go to one of them, in good weather, of course!

Next place eastward on this splendid coast is Dunfanaghy,

a favourite resort of the Irish, but still small and peaceful. I was very impressed with *Arnold's Hotel* and the *Carrig Rua*. Each has its attractions. The first is more spacious, the second has a pleasant bar. *Arnold's* is noted for its connection with pony-trekking holidays, using the hotel as a base. A leaflet and some very detailed notes can be obtained from the hotel. The latter lists everything you need for this type of holiday, and tells you where to buy these items. To whet your appetite for something that is different, if you have not experienced it previously, I quote from the notes:

"If you have never ridden before, this is the time to start, you will be helped and encouraged. All treks are accompanied by an experienced rider who will help trekkers as much as possible. No cantering will be done, and practically no trotting. The rides will be over the surrounding hills, and passing round several lakes. In the mountains, donkeys with their panniers will be seen carrying turf from the bogs. Horn Head, Marble Arch and the Forest and Priory at Ard are visited, and there are rides over the beautiful beaches and sand-dunes." Your weight need not put you off, for: "If you are six stone or sixteen stone, there is a horse for you!" According to the season and accommodation required, these holidays cost from $37.80 to $42.80 a week.

Killyhoey Strand is the nearest beach—a very good one which is also close to Port-na-Blagh, where I particularly like the *Port-na-Blagh Hotel* run by Mr. and Mrs. Dermot Walsh. It overlooks Sheephaven Bay, has lovely views from its lounges, and like the other hotels in the area is well situated for the various amenities, which include golf, tennis, boating, lake and sea fishing. Dancing takes place in the hotel every night during season.

Many tours can be made from here, all of them through fine Donegal country but the really exciting one is a trip

183

along the Atlantic Drive, with the best vista coming at the climax, just before you drop down again to Downings and Rosapenna. To reach the Drive, you go through Creeslough, and as you come out of Port-na-Blagh, you will see a sign to Marble Hill Strand. This is one of the loveliest beaches I have seen—wide, deep and curved, sheltered at both ends. If you stay at the hotel, you will want to spend most of your time here—if you are only driving through, don't miss it. You can also stay at the *Shannon Hotel* above the beach.

Coming off the Atlantic Drive, you will find the *Beach Hotel*, at Downings, also on Sheephaven Bay. This is run by artist Taylor Carson and his wife—he says she does it all herself—and is one of the centres for holidays used by the Irish Landscape School of Painting which I have mentioned in Part One. Close by is the *Rosapenna Hotel*, where there had been a fire and at the time of my visit, two hotels were being built to replace the original. They belong to the same management, and it was planned that one, the *Golf*, would be open by the beginning of the 1964 season, the *Rosapenna* itself by July. Both are in the same grounds overlooking Sheephaven Bay. The *Golf* bedrooms are especially quiet, being separated from the public rooms by the reception area, one wall of which, like one wall of the dining-room, is entirely of glass, giving a clear view.

Extra land has been bought as a landing strip for small private aircraft. The strand is licensed for this purpose, but planes cannot be parked there for fear of submergence due to tide changes at night.

Amenities include a safe, sandy, private beach and a private pool in a rocky cove; an eighteen-hole golf course (nine more holes are in preparation); tennis courts and a croquet lawn; shooting; good salmon and sea trout fishing on Glen Lough and in the Lackagh river. Plans were in hand to provide ponies for trekking, especially around the Errigal and Muckish mountains. Errigal, 2,466 feet, is the highest peak in Donegal.

Nearby is Carrigart, on the Rosguill Peninsula between Sheephaven and Mulroy Bay. The *Carrigart* is a comfortable hotel there, and like the *Beach*, is an artists' haunt. From Carrigart, go southward through Milford to Rathmullan, which may now be better signposted than it was when I was there. In case it is not, look for a sign on a left-hand fork on the road to Rathmelton, of which a short form—Ramelton—is also used. In its own grounds on the shore of Lough Swilly Rathmullan House, very carefully converted into a hotel without losing its original attraction. Well-appointed rooms look out over the lake with the mountains beyond, and there is a half-mile beach right in front of the hotel. The dining room and bar are most pleasant, and the food is very good. Mr. Robert Wheeler, one of the directors of the company which owns this and a small fishermen's hotel at Milford, manages the house himself, and he and his colleagues have done everything possible to create a warm, friendly, house-party atmosphere while still providing unobtrusive efficiency in running the place.

This became one of my favourites. You may well see me there on my holiday when you go. In the grounds, too, close to the beach, there are a few chalets—actually for living in, not merely for use during the day. These are designed specially for families not wishing to stay in the hotel, although they have full use of all its amenities, and can either eat in the hotel or cook for themselves in the chalet "galley". The chalets are completely equipped. There is a baby-sitting service for guests, whether they stay in the hotel or a chalet. You can fish, play tennis or croquet, and golf—the latter on a course two miles away. Across Lough Swilly, there is the Inishowen peninsula to explore. On your way in, you will see a most important

185

ancient monument, the Grianan of Aileach, a circular stone fort on the summit of Greenan Mountain. It is believed to date from about 1700 B.C. and was once the residence of the O'Neill Kings of Ulster.

Rathmullan House was the last place I visited on my tour before crossing the border into Northern Ireland. It left me with very contented impressions of Donegal, and the certainty that I would keep going back.

THE REST OF EIRE

The very nature of Ireland makes it inexhaustible for the tourist who is seeking peace and beauty—which are abundant. So although, in the previous pages, I have covered all the places most people want to see, because these are well-known and conveniently on the main tourist routes, as well as some off the beaten track, you are likely to explore other areas for yourself, and a few pointers to places of interest in the counties not mentioned so far may be helpful. In this final round-up of Eire, I have not included all the castles and round towers, crosses and dolmens as, with the exceptions I have made, most of the important ones are in the areas already described.

GALWAY TO ATHLONE AND DUBLIN

On one of my tours in Ireland, I simply covered the southern part of the south, finishing up at Galway before returning to Dublin via Athlone. There were certainly one or two pleasant surprises on this run. The country around Galway is very flat, the division of fields made mostly by low walls of irregular stones, loosely piled on top of each other. I saw the occasional gypsy camp alongside the road, with canvas-covered hide-outs attached to the horse-drawn caravans, children crouching on the warm dry hay, the smell

186

of peaty fires—and all the appearances of outdoor living in complete confusion! In the fields, the tall corn stooks, evenly-spaced, looked like a live audience in an open-air theatre. Sometimes they reminded me of John Wyndham's science-fiction creatures, "the triffids".

The flat country continues for a few miles but gradually becomes more interesting on the approach to Ballinasloe, seven miles short of which, on the Athenry road, is the Franciscan Kilconnell Abbey. Its well-preserved tower is visible as you approach the village from the west, and bears a small, faded flag with an Irish harp. Founded in 1400, it was restored and enlarged in 1460, and granted to an English settler, Charles Calthorpe, at the time of the dissolution. Much of the very beautiful, serene, creeper-covered building is in perfect condition. Sometimes there are sheep grazing on the gentle slope in front, and you can walk across from the road to see the building closely, or find the caretaker to guide you inside—he lives at the end of the village.

A slight southward diversion *en route* for Ballinasloe would enable you to see the stained glass windows in St. Brendan's Cathedral at Loughrea. Those set back to the right of the altar are the most impressive. Near Loughrea is the ancient Turoe Stone.

According to that well-known fisherman, Bernard Venables, quoted in the little town's leaflet, "the citizens of Ballinasloe have grown accustomed to the earnest angling pilgrims from England". Many readers with highly developed piscatorial senses will need no telling that here, on the River Suck, are facilities for some of the best coarse fishing to be had anywhere. Others can obtain all the information they need, either in advance from the local Angling Association, or when they arrive, in the detailed leaflet I have mentioned.

187

Ballinasloe describes itself as a town of 6,000 people, at the same time a place having the quaintness of a village. You will do well to time your arrival for the lunch-hour, and however much or little you are impressed by the town, take the meal at *Hayden's Hotel*. Frankly, although Ballinasloe is on a main road, it cannot pretend to be located in an exciting position for tourists other than fishermen. Yet the hotel alone puts it on the map of places that just should not be missed. Splendid modern extensions to the building, and bright imaginative contemporary furnishings greet you, as do Mr. Michael O'Carroll and his son, who have turned their establishment into one of the best I have seen on my travels.

If you are a male reader and you go into the restaurant with a pretty girl, put her in a seat where she won't distract your attention from the beautiful black-and-white blown-up photograph of the lower lake at Killarney which, cleverly lit by concealed strips, covers one of the walls. The restaurant has three different kinds of pleasant ceiling lighting, and a loggia along its length facing the garden. The food is superb.

Although Athlone, famous mainly for its radio station and its historical associations, is a pleasant town and important junction, it is not especially interesting to holiday-makers. However, it has given birth to some distinguished citizens, including the world-famous tenor, the late John McCormack, and politician-journalist the late T. P. O'Connor. Oliver Goldsmith went to school in Athlone, and lived for many years at Lissoy, nine miles from the town and inspiration for his poem "The Deserted Village". For three weeks in the early summer, Athlone is the scene of the National Drama Festival, and is generally very active in the cultural field.

Two of the town's modern hotels must be mentioned. In

the *Prince of Wales*, you can be sure of good food, and if you do stay there, you will find all rooms have radio and telephone, as well as thermostatically controlled convector heating. Those on the second and third floors have balconies. One thing that impressed me was the ample car park, a boon in the centre of any town.

An inn which once catered for the horse and carriage business of the latter part of the eighteenth century and became *Garty's Hotel* in 1821, is now the *Royal Hotel*. Dryly humorous, its brochure calls the transformation of the hotel the result of anxiety "not to compete with, but to surpass the many first class hotels available to visitors to Ireland". Successful in that aim or not, the hotel certainly offers a great deal of comfort in a pleasant atmosphere. It also has a big ballroom on the second floor.

If you are stopping off here even without staying, you can shop at the Jersey Boutique in Court Devenish by the old castle of that name; and two places worth visiting outside town are Lough Ree and the important Clonmacnois archaeological site, eight miles southward.

The route from Athlone to Dublin is normally through Kinnegad; Maynooth, well-known for St. Patrick's College, main training centre of Catholic diocesan clergy in Ireland; and Leixlip, one mile south-west of which is the Wonderful Barn, built in 1743 by Lady Louisa Connolly of Castletown, to relieve distress caused by famine. The building is a conical brick and stone structure, has five storeys of single rooms with domed ceilings. Around the exterior is a spiral stairway of stone, giving access to all the floors and the point of the cone, from which there is a good view of the countryside. A short distance north of the road between Maynooth and Celbridge to the south-east is Connolly's Folly, a strange obelisk built by the same lady for the same purpose.

If you have time to divert from Kinnegad on your way to the capital, you can go through Trim, see its castle, and head for the historically famous Boyne Valley. At the mouth of the river is Drogheda, which Cromwell took in 1649, when he massacred both the garrison and inhabitants, and which surrendered to William after the Battle of the Boyne. There are bathing, hunting and golfing all close to the town, and the Boyne is one of the best salmon rivers in the country. Two miles from the point at which it is joined by the River Mattock is Mellifont Abbey, where the foliage-covered remains of "The Lavabo" are an unusual sight. Five miles away at Monasterboice is Muireadach's Cross, one of the most important examples of its kind of early Christian art in the country. In the valley, too, is ancient Tara, seat of the high-kings, although on its hill there is now little to see, apart from a few circular ramparts and mounds.

Six miles south of the border is *Ballymacscanlon House Hotel*, an excellent place at which to dine or stay, either on your way into Northern Ireland or after crossing back into Eire. For fifty years, it was the home of the Plunkett family, and while its exterior has been retained, it has been cleverly modernised inside. It offers a great deal of comfort in quiet grounds of 300 acres. There are tennis courts and a putting green; golf, fishing and bathing facilities are within easy reach.

The district around Ballymacscanlon was inhabited in the pre-historic era. Among important archaeological remains is the Proleck Stone or Giant's Load, said to have been erected by a giant named Porrah Buagh Mac Shagan. This fiction provides an answer to a fact—that, somehow the huge stone at the top, weighing over 46 tons, was put there to rest on three slender supports more than six feet high. The monument is believed to date from the Bronze Age, about 4000 B.C. Nearby, on Faughart Hill, is an old church, the cemetery of which is claimed to be the resting place of Edward Bruce, King of Ireland, brother of Robert the Bruce. Before the middle of the eighteenth century, a spring on the north side of Ballymacscanlon village was well-known for its curative properties, and among the people who came to seek cures in 1720 was an old man said to have been completely restored in health after being bedridden for more than 10 years.

KILDARE

As well as the barn at Leixlip, the College at Maynooth, there are the Japanese Gardens on the Tully estate outside Kildare town. These were set out by a designer brought over from Japan, and they tell the story of man from cradle to grave, beginning with the Cave of Birth, from which the tiny Stepping Stones of Childhood lead to a dark cave which represents the child's lack of understanding. Beyond here are the Hill of Learning, the Unguarded Pitfall, the Island of Joy and Wonder, the Bridge of Matrimony, and so on. The gardens are open from 2.30 to 6 p.m. on Sundays, Holy Days and Bank Holidays, from April to mid-October, admission 12 c. There is also a miniature village, shaped from volcanic lava. Tully is the home of the Irish National Stud, where many modern methods and ideas have been introduced. The Stud Managers' Course held there is the first of its kind in Europe, probably in the world.

TIPPERARY

At Cashel, not to be confused with the place of the same name in Connemara, is the famous Rock of Cashel, looming over the town, and on top of which are some fine ruins on what is one of the country's most important historic sites.

191

It was the seat of the Munster kings from about A.D. 370 to 1101. The Round Tower, 92 feet high, and believed to be tenth century, is a perfect specimen. There is also the unique Cross of St. Patrick which, when complete, formed a cross enclosed in a frame, without the characteristic ring around the intersection. The buildings are sometimes floodlit.

Two miles west of Cashel, on the River Suir, there is good salmon and trout fishing, and several tributaries hold trout. As long ago as 1899, in his book *Fly Fishing*, Viscount Gray of Falloden wrote: "I can imagine that in May and June it might be the finest dry fly fishing in the United Kingdom." Although subsequent history made his statement inaccurate, anglers are still well rewarded by the Suir. North of Cashel, too, at Thurles, is *Hayes' Hotel*, a good centre for fly fishers only (preferably dry fly) and visitors to which will find the waters available at the Anglers' Association charge of 60 c. a day per rod, or $3.60 a week including Sunday. Facilities also exist at Clonmel, which borders on the Comeragh Mountains area I have described elsewhere. Clonmel was the birthplace of Laurence Sterne, author of *Tristram Shandy* and was the headquarters of Bianconi, who introduced the stagecoach into Ireland. The town is pleasantly situated.

KILKENNY

One of two "sister" rivers to the Suir is the Barrow, also in a lovely, quiet fishing and boating district. An especially beautiful spot is Graignamanagh, on a bend of the river where Brandon Hill provides the background. If you climb the hill (1,694 feet) you will have a view which takes in both the Barrow valley and that of the other "sister" river, the Nore. The Barrow is salmon and trout water. All coarse fishing is free. Seán O'Faoláin wrote of this area: "Stand

192

20. Tranarossan
    Bay,
    Co. Donegal

21. Fishing at
    Clones,
    Co. Monaghan

22. The ruins of Dunluce Castle, Co. Antrim

23. The Giant's
    Causeway,
    Co. Antrim

24. Ballintoy, Co.
    Antrim

25. The beach at Ballycastle, Co. Antrim

26. Glenariff, loveliest of the Glens of Antrim

on any height and look far and wide over the valley, and you at once sense both its wealth and its seclusion. You see a rolling terrain threaded by the winding river rising to far hills chequered by blond cornfields and the varying green of many crops. The whole valley swoons in an air of tranquillity so that on still days even the clouds lie asleep across the distant mountains and one gets an overpowering sensation of a peace as unbroken as the buzzing of bees."

Graignamanagh town takes its name from the Cistercian Abbey of which English writer John Bernard Trotter, who saw the ruins in 1812, said: "I cannot describe how nobly venerable it looked. I do not except the celebrated Abbey of Tintern in Monmouthshire, when I say that nothing could be found more venerable and beautifully interesting in the Empire than Graignamanagh Abbey." The church, one of the few in Ireland founded over 750 years ago, is still in use. Within the walls, you can see an odd, cross-legged figure of a knight in armour, locally known as "Strongbow", and the partly restored Processional Door, bearing fine examples of thirteenth-century stone carving.

CAVAN AND MONAGHAN

On a leaflet published by the Cavan District Tourist Association, I read: "We are particular that intending visitors get a complete picture of the district before arrival. You are requested to write to our Secretary who will supply all the necessary information. Visitors on arrival are also requested to contact our Secretary, who will give more up-to-date information." After telling you that his name is Hugh Gough, and his address is 4 MacDermott Street, Cavan, I could leave the rest to him. But that would be a little unfair. In fact, Cavan is beautiful lake country providing good coarse fishing. Lough Sheelin and Annagh

Lake offer trout fishing. Lough Oughter is the main water area, its lakes blending into each other being connected by small rivers. There are several good fishing lakes around Bailieborough in East Cavan. Monaghan, too, is excellent fishing country. There are a dozen lakes stocked with bream, pike, perch, roach and trout. Carrickmacross makes a convenient centre.

THE ISLANDS

Apart from the Aran Islands and others described in the text so far, the following are worth noting. Off-shore from the Dingle Peninsula in County Kerry are the seven islands and numerous rocks known as the Blasket islands. In the village of Dunquin, you can hire a curragh to take you over. You can go to Clare Island, a few miles south of Achill (see page 172) on the motor-boat that takes the mail from Roonah Quay. Clare was the headquarters of sea-queen Grace O'Malley. She is buried in the island abbey, which dates from 1224, and the big square castle that was her home overlooks the little harbour.

You can also hire a motorboat at Burtonport in Donegal to take you the three-mile journey to Aranmore, which has wonderful cliff scenery, some interesting caves, and the ten-room *Glen Hotel*. The hotel provides transport, is fully licensed, serves *à la carte* meals. Aranmore is a good place for anyone interested in wild life—there are grey seals and many kinds of seabirds around its shores. Five miles off the north-western coast of Donegal is Tory Island, its grim appearance a reflection of the rough seas sometimes encountered on the boat trip. Although the outward journey may be smooth, you can be temporarily stranded on the island, but with the consolation of meeting some of the hospitable inhabitants, who number over 200. Their boats are even more fascinating than the Aran curraghs.

Tory Island canoes have blunt prows, no seats, and are manipulated with paddles.

Inishmurray Island, in County Sligo, shares with Tory the distinction of having no rats, but unlike Tory, is also minus inhabitants. This is the result of progress, not the fact that during World War I, a British destroyer mistook its shape for that of a German submarine and let off a torpedo which scared everyone on the island. Inishmurray contains numerous early Christian relics. A boat can be hired to take you there from Grange, above Sligo town.

PART FOUR

NORTHERN IRELAND

GENERAL INFORMATION

Although Northern Ireland is often called Ulster, the province actually consists of the Six Counties which are part of the United Kingdom, and three—Donegal, Cavan and Monaghan—which belong to Eire.

Before going to Ireland, it is hard to imagine what the division between north and south means, but the differences are undeniable. Once you have been there, you will make your own assessment of certain aspects which it is not the purpose of a guidebook to emphasise.

In terms of tourism, it is probably fair to say that while resorts like Bangor, Ballycastle, Newcastle, Portrush and Portstewart are highly developed, much more has to be done to provide amenities in certain beauty spots—like Lough Erne—without spoiling their natural attractions. I am very much in favour of preserving and protecting places, and this the Northern Ireland Government will do, while making it easier, with improvements in signposting, for visitors to find and see them.

I think there is a need for more hotels in the middle category, although the Northern Ireland authorities claim that, for the size of their area, they have more—and more guest and boarding houses—than there are in the south. Without going further into this question, I am sure you will enjoy all the highspots I have pinpointed and, in all probability, find that some if not all of the proposals for developing the north will have been implemented by the time you read this book.

The central feature in the Arms of Ulster is a Red Hand, and the Belfast Museum staff constantly receive queries as to whether the hand should be dexter (right) or sinister (left). Many people make indiscriminate use of the device for all kinds of purposes, ranging from a position on a menu card to one on a ship's funnel and, although the correct hand to use has been indicated from time to time, use of the wrong one is persistent. For this reason, the Belfast Museum and Art Gallery Bulletin, in 1951, published a helpful note, quoting one written by the late John Vinycomb, M.R.I.A., in his time a leading authority on heraldic devices. He wrote:

". . . The arms assigned to the Province of Ulster, and registered in the Office of Ulster King of Arms, are in plain terms—a red cross upon a gold field, with a small white shield bearing a red right hand cut off at the wrist, placed on the centre of the cross. These arms are derived from those borne by De Burgo, Earl of Ulster of the period of the Norman invasion, with the addition of the O'Neill escutcheon. As to the origin of the celebrated device of the Red Hand, much has been written. The early legend of the cutting off of the left hand, and throwing it ashore is not of any account, for the same story appears in many places, and is not borne out by the fact that the O'Neills, Kings of Ulster, and all branches of that princely house invariably used the right hand as do the present representatives. All the early seals of the O'Neills have the right hand—never the left.

"The reason of the confusion as to right or left hand appears to have arisen in this way: On the institution of the Order of Baronets of Ulster by King James I 'a hand gules' was adopted as the badge of the new Order (right or left not specified). A dexter or a sinister hand was used indiscriminately by the baronets for some time, but gradually settled down exclusively to the sinister hand—the ancient legend apparently carrying the day as regards the badge of the baronetcy. As the badge of the province, however, the dexter is the right hand, in a double sense, and is by authority so recorded in Ulster's Office. And so it remains that the badge of the province —'The Red Hand of O'Neill'—argent a dexter hand gules—is authoritatively settled beyond dispute. There should be no drops of blood."

Mr. Vinycomb also adapted old lines on "The Rule of the Road" to explain which hand to use, under the title, "Right versus left." These read as follows:

"The Red Hand of Ulster's a paradox quite,
    To Baronets 'tis said to belong;
If they use the left hand, they're sure to be right,
    And to use the right hand would be wrong,
For the Province, a different custom applies,
    And just the reverse is the rule;
If you use the right hand you'll be right, safe and wise,
    If you use the left hand you're a fool."

THE NATIONAL TRUST

The Northern Ireland Committee of the National Trust has a considerable number of historically interesting or attractive houses, gardens and beauty spots in its care.

Houses and gardens have been mentioned at the appropriate places in the text covering the areas in which they are located, beauty spots—apart from the Giant's Causeway, Whitepark Bay and Cushenden village, all in the care of the Trust—are indicated below. The latter are open to the public at all times, of course, and without charge. Admission to houses and gardens, for 18 c. in some cases, 30 c. in others, is during restricted hours, of which, as they are variable, details are best obtained in the various areas when you reach them.

The dates of opening are also variable according to season, and some properties are closed at certain periods for maintenance. Normally, most are open all the year round. The following summary of the others is taken from a booklet published by the National Trust, Northern Ireland Committee, 82 Dublin Road, Belfast, with whom arrangements can be made for special parties outside ordinary hours of opening. Address enquiries to the Secretary.

Tuesday:	Castlecoole, Florence Court, Springhill, Mountstewart Gardens
Wednesday:	Castlecoole, Florence Court, Springhill, Rowallane, Castleward, Derrymore, Ardress House
Thursday:	Mountstewart Gardens, Derrymore, Ardress House
Friday:	Castlecoole, Florence Court, Springhill
Saturday:	All properties
Sunday:	Rowallane; and July-September, Castlecoole, Florence Court, Springhill, Ardress House
Monday Bank Holidays:	All properties

Beauty Spots. As in the case of the Mussenden Temple overlooking Magilligan Strand at Downhill, mentioned in the text, other places to which there is free access at all times are:

Minnowburn Beeches, on the outskirts of Belfast
Lisnabreeny, two miles south of the capital
Collin Glen, also on the outskirts of Belfast
Ballymacormick Point, near Groomsport
Killynether, near Newtownards
Ballymoyer, near Newry

National Trust Tours. In the 1964 season, the Trust organised special seven-day coach tours of gardens, lakes and sea coast, one of which took in the Castlecoole and Florence Court properties. Details can be obtained from the offices at the above address.

*　　*　　*

HOMES OF UNITED STATES PRESIDENTS

At the time of writing, the Northern Ireland Government was negotiating for the purchase of two old houses associated with American Presidents of Ulster origin. American visitors may be interested to see the properties which are at Cullybackey, near Ballymena, in County Antrim, and at Dergalt, near Strabane, in County Tyrone.

The Cullybackey house was the home in which William Arthur (father of President Chester Allan Arthur) lived before emigrating to America about 1816. The Dergalt house was the home of James Wilson (grandfather of President Woodrow Wilson) before he emigrated to the States about 1807. It is still occupied by a branch of the Wilson family.

Thirteen presidents of the United States were of Ulster descent.

ANCIENT MONUMENTS

It will be appreciated that not all of Northern Ireland's ancient monuments can be detailed here, although quite a number, including the more important castles, have been mentioned. Anyone particularly interested in detailed information should note that publications by H.M. Stationery Office and available from its branches in London, Belfast, Manchester, Birmingham, Bristol and Edinburgh, include *Ancient Monuments of Northern Ireland, Vol. I: In State Care;* several guides to individual monuments in this category; a booklet entitled *Ancient Monuments in Northern Ireland not in State Charge;* and some archaeological research papers.

IRISH LINEN

Residents of London and visitors from abroad who know the Irish Linen shop in Bond Street may or may not be among them, but many people all over the world write to ask the Irish Linen Guild and the Irish linen industry generally for literature.

The Guild, which has offices at 91 Oxford Street, London, W.1 (Tel.: REGent 6549) publishes a useful illustrated booklet which touches on the historical aspect, describes the manufacture of linen, and draws attention to its use by young Irish designer Sybil Connolly and those who have been famous much longer, such as Charles Creed and Digby Morton.

Lynn Usitat, textile trade magazine editor, is the author of a very entertaining booklet on linen, published by H. R. Carter, Ltd., Saxone House, Donegall Place, Belfast (price 3s. 6d., or 50 cents in the U.S.A. and Canada).

He begins with biblical references to linen and its manufacture by the Egyptians and the Children of Israel, uses recent discoveries in Egypt, and examples like the Bayeux tapestry to underline the lasting qualities of the material, points out that Shakespeare continually mentions linen with affection in his plays, goes on to give the Celtic origins of the actual name, linen. Other sections of the booklet tell of the time "When Linen Went to War", "Flax Culture and Retting", "Tow Preparation and Spinning", as well as weaving, bleaching, dyeing and finishing.

The annual production of the Irish linen industry is 100 million square yards.

Visitors are welcome at the "Old Bushmills" Distillery, Co. Antrim, where the only pure malt whiskey in Ireland is made. The distillery is set in pleasant country, which is described in Part Four, and about which some lively tales are contained in a little booklet published by the company. The original grant to distil whiskey at Bushmills was made in 1608; between 1883 and 1908 the brand received ten awards.

ANGLING

As in Eire, the scope for anglers in Northern Ireland is very considerable, being all the more concentrated in the smaller area, where one is never far from fishing grounds. Species in Ulster include both game (salmon, sea trout and brown trout) and coarse (pike, perch, rudd, bream, roach and eels). Angling for the latter is permitted throughout the year, as there is no close season for coarse fish. The game fish season usually lasts from the beginning of April to the end of September, although certain waters open on 1st March and do not close until 31st October.

Rod Licence Fees. Salmon and sea trout anglers must take out the appropriate Statutory Rod Licence, costing either $3.60 or $4.80 a season according to locality and which covers the holder for angling for any other species of fish without any further cost. For coarse fish, the rod licence is $1.20 a season except in one locality where no licence fee is levied for any species apart from salmon or sea-trout.

Salmon Waters. Lough Melvin receives runs of spring salmon, but the bulk of salmon in Northern Ireland belongs to the grilse family (average weight 5 to 7 lbs.) which enter the fresh water about mid-June, if the rains have been obliging. Sufficient quantities for good sport are usually in the rivers by mid-July. Among the main waters favoured by the salmon are:

CO. ANTRIM	Rivers Maine, Braid, Glenwherry, Clough, Bush and Dun
CO. DOWN	Rivers Shimna and Quoile (Mourne Mountains district)
CO. ARMAGH	River Blackwater
CO. FERMANAGH	Rivers Arney and Colebrooke; Loughs Erne and Melvin
CO. TYRONE	Rivers Mourne, Strule, Derg, Glenelly and Ballinderry
CO. DERRY	Rivers Bann (lower), Moyola, Roe and Faughan

Not all these waters are free—some are strictly preserves of clubs, associations or syndicates, but several of these issue tickets to visitors at an average daily cost of $1.20 to $2.40. On certain stretches no ticket is necessary.

Sea-Trout Waters. With the exception of those in Co. Fermanagh, all the above salmon waters also receive runs of sea-trout from around mid-June onwards, the average weight being about 1 lb. Conditions covering the issue of tickets for salmon also apply to sea-trout. In one water, there is free sea-trout fishing. This is Strangford Lough, which is salt water, and where large shoals of sea-trout have been found between March and May in the last few years. Specimens of 2 to 4½ lbs. have been caught on spinning baits by shore-based anglers.

Brown Trout. Brown trout are found in countless rivers, streams, burns, lakes and ponds. Many weigh ½ to 1 lb., but in more than one water, specimens of 10 lbs. and more have been caught. Lough Erne is one of these—5-pounders are frequently caught here, many are between 8 and 13 lbs., and the biggest in recent years was 16½ lbs., caught by an angler who in 1963 took a total of 420 big trout from the

Lough. This water is best fished from a boat. Several can be hired, with or without boatmen, for not more than $5 a day. I have mentioned in Part Four the accommodation available to anglers at Enniskillen, on Lough Erne. Big trout are also found in feeder rivers like the Colebrooke and the Arney, especially in late summer. Lough Melvin is noted for Gillaroo and Sonaghan Trout, Lough Neagh feeder streams for really big trout, especially the heavyweight Dollaghan. Ordinary brown trout are found in the Belfast district reservoirs, and a visitor's ticket covering all of these is available for $7.50 a season. A rod licence fee—costing $1.20 a season—is essential for brown trout angling throughout Northern Ireland except in the area of the Foyle Fisheries Commission, but this fee is not payable by anglers who hold the local Statutory Rod Licence for salmon and/or sea-trout.

Coarse Fishing. Because game fishing is so abundant, Northern Ireland anglers have little time for coarse species, believing that if these did not reside in Ulster waters, there would be far greater stocks of trout and salmon. Accordingly, visitors who prefer coarse fishing are welcome to catch fish which local rods despise and which, because they do, can be caught in plenty. Strong tackle is recommended as although, normally unmolested, the fish fall unsuspectingly for the bait, they react fiercely when they feel the hook and a big specimen can smash light tackle.

Bait. Maggots are not available in Ulster shops. Anglers who use this bait should take their own. Not all the varieties of ground-bait are available, but there is a choice of pollards, pig meal, Indian meal and barley meal, stocked locally for the requirements of the agricultural community.

Coarse Fish Rivers. An angler who wants to vary lough fishing with river fishing can travel, for instance, the few miles from Enniskillen to Lisnaskea, where he will have

207

miles of the river Colebrooke to himself and in many stretches find pike, rudd and roach. The best roach fishing is at Omagh, 28 miles from Enniskillen. Also, 3½ miles from Omagh is Lough Muck, a small lake holding no game fish, but full of pike, perch and rudd, where no rod licence fee is required, and no boat is needed to fish there. A few roach may also be found, as the 4½ cwt. caught by English rods in 1961 were transferred here. There is another small lake on the Castledillon estate, two miles from Armagh, where fishing for pike and rudd can be enjoyed for sixpence —the stamp duty on an indemnifying agreement between the angler and the lake-owners, who are the Hospitals Authority. Average catch of pike weighs 7 to 10 lbs., although a 20-lb. fish is sometimes caught. Rudd are plentiful but not large.

Other Coarse Fishing Waters. Some other coarse fishing waters will be found at: Lough Neagh (on the shores)— pike and bream; Toombridge—large pike; the River Maine—pike; River Blackwater—pike and bream; Clea Lough—pike and perch; River Quoile—perch; River Bann—pike; River Lagan—pike and perch; Camlough— bream, perch and rudd; and Lough Ross—big pike. There are many more.

Warning on Wading. Many waters are literally virgin, having yet to see an angling bait. Care should be exercised in approaching some, especially those with a deep fringe of reeds along the perimeter, where the going can be soft and treacherous. On no occasion should wading be considered unless the angler has been assured of safety.

Angling Information Source. It should be noted that Ulster waters are essentially pleasure fishing grounds, for which reason competitions, even for game fish, are rare. Enniskillen is the only centre at which coarse fish angling competitions are promoted.

A list of available accommodation for anglers, details of centres, travel facilities, species, rod licences and other facilities can be obtained from The Information Centre, Northern Ireland Tourist Board, 6 Royal Avenue, Belfast, Northern Ireland.

WATER SPORTS

Water ski-ing and power-boat racing, shows, demonstrations and competitions are held on Lough Henney, a natural arena with surrounding hills on which spectators can park their cars and from which they have an excellent view.

On Monday evenings and weekends at Lough Henney, the Meteor Water-Ski Club holds special classes for beginners. The charge is $2.40 a night, working out at less than the international rate of 12 c. a minute. Details can be obtained from the vice-chairman of the Club: Ken McCormick, 16 Shrewsbury Park, Belfast 9. Tel.: (Daytime) 30231, (Night) 660364.

Power-boat racing also takes place on Lough Aghery. Both lakes are just off the main Belfast-Newcastle road. Take the second turning right after passing Temple Crossroads, going south from Belfast. Strangford Lough is another water on which water ski-ing and power boat racing and demonstrations take place during the regatta season.

The Belfast Branch of the British Sub-Aqua Club has a programme of diving, spearfishing and general training which, from May onwards, also includes expeditions to see the wrecks off the north Antrim coast. Members also dive for clams on the bed of Strangford Lough, go lobster and spearfishing off the Donegal coast. The Club welcomes visitors and charges are nominal. Details are obtainable from: Vernon Collier, Sinclair's Ltd., 89–101 Royal Avenue, Belfast 1.

Mountaineering enthusiasts can obtain information about the Mourne School of Mountaineering from the Information Centre of the Northern Ireland Tourist Board, 10 Royal Avenue, Belfast. Details of courses organised by the Central Council of Physical Recreation can be obtained from their offices: Northern Ireland Secretary, C.C.P.R., 49 Malone Road, Belfast 9.

The Tourist Board, in co-operation with the Irish Mountaineering Club, are the publishers of a booklet by Dr. P. W. F. Gribbon, called *Mourne Rock Climbs.*

EVENTS

Numerous events of many kinds fill the Northern Ireland calendar. Apart from those I have mentioned elsewhere in the text, among the interesting ones are the May Fair at Ballyclare; the Royal Ulster Agricultural Show at Belfast, also in May; the motor-cycling "North-West 200" on the Portrush-Portstewart-Coleraine circuit at the end of May; the colourful Orangemen's Display at Belfast on 12th July; the Donkey Derby near Enniskillen, and the International Ulster Grand Prix on the Dundrod circuit, near Belfast, both in August. Go-kart racing can be seen at Portrush. It also takes place in the show grounds at Ballymena. On a serious note, there is the St. Patrick's Day pilgrimage to Saul.

A TOUR OF NORTHERN IRELAND

1. ULSTER LAKELAND—COUNTY FERMANAGH

If you happen to be following the same itinerary as I did, heading from County Sligo for Donegal—and provided you are driving your own car—you can cross into Northern Ireland at Belleek, either to see the famous pottery there, or visit Lough Erne, or both. You can then cross out again to Donegal and re-enter near Londonderry or, if Donegal is not on your itinerary (which would be a pity) continue your tour in the north.

Looking at its forbidding exterior, no-one would know that there are light and airy workshops inside the Belleek pottery where, instead of the machine-age clangour, visitors will find patient craftsmen, in a peaceful atmosphere, quietly fashioning the delicate and beautiful pieces which are world-famous.

The pottery was founded in 1857, when a visiting industrialist was fascinated by the colour of the whitewash on a country house. He found that the nearby hills contained considerable supplies of the materials necessary to the manufacture of china. Mines were opened, so was the pottery, which began making some of the most exclusive products of this kind, in a place where, despite what are now thought to be the highest production costs in the country, there are no "seconds". A piece bearing the slightest flaw is smashed instantly.

On a 25-minute tour—visitors are very welcome—you can see the various stages of production, which starts with the grinding of the raw materials into creamy clay. After being drained of impurities, the material is poured into moulds and quickly sets. The artistic craftsmen take up their work at this point, preparing the raw china for the first firing—in the electric ovens, a modern item which has replaced the big coal-fired kilns used for nearly a hundred years. Glazing and another baking take place before the artists really get to work. Designs are taken from the tracery of ornamentation in the Book of Kells, the ancient Irish manuscript which I have mentioned elsewhere in the text. Many new designs have been introduced in recent years. More firing, painting and finishing complete the processes.

I was fascinated, as all visitors are, by the touch of the artists who apply tiny flowers to the various pieces, and by the fact that the familiar trellis basket is made from very pliable china clay which is put through a machine to emerge looking rather like strips of spaghetti. Belleek china is exported all over the world, its main markets being Australia, Canada, New Zealand, South Africa and the United States.

Assuming you are going on to see Lough Erne, and possibly to stop in Enniskillen for a night, make the pleasant run down the west side of Lower Lough Erne, with the idea of driving out on the east side if you are moving on to Donegal. This is the most suitable route even if you are remaining in the north.

I shall always remember Enniskillen as the town where, when a fire occurs, it is reported to the police station, at which a siren is started to call out the auxiliary fire brigade, who cut it off at their end when they respond. When you go there, you will have certain advantages over me. Stay as I did at the *Imperial Hotel*, where an excellent conversion should now be complete. Efficient use has been made of the upper floor space, especially in the single rooms, and I was well victualled and serviced in the fine new restaurant. The hotel is constantly used by fishermen, in waters very near the hotel, and the management publishes an angling brochure giving details of the boats, baits, tackle and packed lunches which are part of its service. Winter visitors should note that the bedrooms are centrally heated.

Enniskillen is a river-island town standing between Lower and Upper Lough Erne. An ancient stronghold of the Maguires, rulers of County Fermanagh, the town was incorporated by charter of James I in 1612 and settled by English families. West of the town, on the lakeside, is Portora Royal School, a building mostly dating from 1777, and where the Reverend Lyte, author of "Abide with Me",

212

and Oscar Wilde were pupils. Enniskillen, of course, is the town of the two famous regiments, the Inniskilling Dragoon Guards, and the Royal Inniskilling Fusiliers.

In 1,500 acres of wooded grounds on the east side of the town is Castlecoole, family mansion of the Earls of Belmore, the seventh of whom sold it to the National Trust nine years before his death in 1960, and which is open to the public. It is a fine Georgian house, the work of James Wyatt, and built from Portland stone, the huge blocks of which were taken ten miles by bullock cart to Lough Erne and then by water to Enniskillen. The house is in beautiful condition, not merely of itself, but also because it is very well maintained under the supervision of a new caretaker who had taken over just before my visit. There are lovely grounds in which the walled garden, not being a part of the National Trust property, is closed to the public. The park also contains the local golf course.

Not much remains of Enniskillen Castle, but two miles north of the town, on Devenish Island in Lower Lough Erne, there is an important group of ecclesiastical structures, on the site of a sixth-century monastery. These include the Round Tower, one of the most perfect examples in the country, and bearing sculptured decoration not normally found on such buildings. There is also an interesting Celtic Cross, and other ruins are St. Mary's Abbey and Teampall Mor, the Great Church. North of Devenish, on White Island, the ruins of another small church will be found, as well as remains on other islands, of which there are many in the lake.

Eight miles north of Enniskillen, on the east side of the lake, is Killadeas village, where boats can be hired to visit the islands. The church at Killadeas has some strange carved stones thought to date from the seventh or eighth century, and incorporates remains of the ancient "Yellow Church" which once stood on the site, perhaps even in the time of the religious community of the Culdees or Ceile-De, who owned the lands for many years. Opposite, on the other side of the road, is the smallest Methodist church in use in Ireland.

Here, too, is the former Manor House of the Killadeas estate, now a hotel of that name. The accommodation is unpretentious and the place had not been fully developed at the time of my visit, although I gathered improvements could be expected. It makes a good base for fishermen after the salmon and trout in Lough Erne as well as the other lakes and rivers. Boats and a launch can be hired, gillies, too, and you can go water ski-ing opposite Hay Island in the bay in front of the hotel. There is also shooting in the area. During the last war, the house was requisitioned and used as headquarters for the Killadeas seaplane base, a plane from which sighted the *Bismarck* and facilitated its destruction.

Two miles beyond the hotel, in the second turning on the left, which leads to a point at the lakeside, is the farm of Brian Maguire, descendant of the Maguire kings of Fermanagh. In his workshop, his late brother Hugh, an invalid, made beautiful violins as a hobby. Two of them were displayed at a rural industries development exhibition in Belfast in 1963 and, while it would be unkind to bother him unduly, Mr. Maguire will gladly show them to anyone really interested. Continuing along the main road, past the Castle Archdale forest sign, take the next turning left, a little way along which, from a rise in the road, is one of the finest views of the lake, with White Island in the foreground. This road, which, like the main one, leads to Kesh, will be better signposted by the time you read this book—improvements all round were in hand when I was there.

On the road to Pettigo (where you re-cross the border if you are going up to Donegal before continuing your tour in Northern Ireland) is Irvinestown, near which there are numerous small lakes holding game and coarse fish. *Mahon's Hotel* caters for fishermen using the town as a base, makes a speciality of packed luncheons. Ponies for trekking are also available here.

West of Enniskillen is Lower Lough MacNean, which attracted me very much indeed. From the Marlbank Scenic Loop road above, there is a wonderful view of the lake, and its islands, Cushrush and Inishee. At one end, there is a road on a strip of land which leads to Belcoo, but do not make the mistake of using it, as if you do so, you will have unwittingly crossed the border into Eire, at one of several unapproved points which occur around the country. The border is not marked here at all, but is officially closed, although I understood negotiations for its opening were in hand and may have been successful by now. You cannot take the risk of crossing because, at some later checkpoint, it will be seen that your papers were not stamped.

Near Derrylin, from Cornaleck Point on Upper Lough Erne, facing Nann Island, you can see an attractive home with a boathouse on the far side. The owner regularly swims across to post and collect mail, even in February. This part of the lake, like other areas I have mentioned, will probably be well signposted by the time you go there, and rowing boats, perhaps outboards, will be available for hire. Further up on the far side of the upper lake there is a new fishing chalet. There are interesting remains at Lisnaskea, named after the tree under which the Maguires were inaugurated.

Fermanagh has its own Tourist Development Association, like the County Council keen to protect their unspoiled and beautiful region while opening it to appreciative tourists who will be content with the more peaceful kind of amenities.

215

The area already draws increasing numbers of fishermen and development generally will hinge on a proposal to open up the former R.A.F. aerodrome at St. Angelo. Derby Aviation were very interested in this venture when I was there, and hoped to operate services for the 1965 season. This can be checked with your travel agent, the airline itself, the Ulster office in Lower Regent Street, or at the British Travel and Holidays Association in St. James's Street.

The airfield would also assist visitors to the surrounding regions of Eire, particularly Donegal, and this and other aspects of development have been covered very thoroughly in "Ulster Lakeland", a survey carried out by the Northern Ireland Ministry of Health and Local Government, with the aim of assisting Fermanagh County Council to protect amenities and develop tourist traffic. Published by H.M. Stationery Office, the survey was combined with detailed and carefully worked-out proposals, at least some of which may be implemented by now.

Apart from County Clare, Fermanagh has the only other really interesting cave-systems, of which the most important is Marble Arch. The path leading to this one is almost impassable in places, but at the time of writing, there was a plan to improve it by extension from the upper end of the glen to join the Marlbank road. Marble Arch is nine miles south-west of Enniskillen, and another system also worth exploring—a complex one—is at Boho, seven miles west of the town. There are other caves to explore, as well as caverns and potholes.

Not far from Marble Arch is Florence Court, another National Trust property, the architect of which is unknown —a pity in view of its magnificence, although some of the façades are quite simple because, the story goes, funds became short before the house was completed. Like Castlecoole, it is open to the public.

I moved on from Fermanagh into Donegal, for a tour which I have described elsewhere in the book, and afterwards crossed back into Northern Ireland near Londonderry, or Derry as it is usually called. My visit to this city which, apart from quite a pleasant shopping area, and its ancient walls with their elevated walkway, has little to interest the tourist, is memorable for two things. One was the Easter wedding party that completely blocked the entrance to the hotel on my arrival—when the bridegroom struggled into the middle of the road trying to evade two female guests intent on stuffing confetti down the seat of his trousers—and the other was the hotel itself.

Aside from its unfortunate name—*The City*—it has a fine new wing with well-appointed friendly rooms, and a restaurant where, in candlelight, on non-summer Saturdays, you can enjoy a quartet with a good beat playing nostalgia-period music for dinner-dancing, and a most attentive staff steers you through seven courses of well-prepared food. There is plenty of choice on the imaginative menu, and one way and another, it is not surprising that *The City* is the social centre of the city.

Skirting Lough Foyle, perhaps diverting first to see the Rough Fort, an old ring fort, a mile west of Limavady, you come to the coast and, before Portstewart, the two little resorts of Downhill and Castlerock. Downhill is near the centre of Magilligan Strand, a splendid six-mile beach. If you ever wondered who inspired so many owners all over Europe to call their hotels "Bristol" you will be interested to know that it was the Earl of Bristol, Bishop of Derry, who built the Mussenden Temple on a clifftop above Magilligan. Designed on the lines of the Temples of Vesta in Rome and Tivoli, it was used as a library and served as a kind of summer-house to Downhill Castle (now in ruins, although the entrance gates still stand). The interior of the Temple, which is in the care of the National Trust, has suffered so considerably from the elements that restoration has proved impossible, but the exterior is a good example of a classical folly, in this case with a dramatic setting. It dates from 1783.

Castlerock is also near Magilligan Strand, has its own beach with safe bathing and is backed by big sand dunes. Amenities include a golf course and sea-trout angling. There are two hotels and a guest house. Downhill has one hotel.

Portstewart, where there are four licensed and five unlicensed hotels, as well as a dozen guest houses and some boarding houses, is a small resort which I liked very much. With respect to the residents concerned, I think it is a pity that their homes have developed into a dormitory area on the approach to the fine beach, which is very attractive in its setting overlooking the bay, with views of the mouth of Lough Foyle and the Donegal coast. Cars can be driven to any part of the beach. Apart from bathing on the beach, there are enclosed pools by the promenade, golf, tennis, boating and angling facilities, and the little resort has a favourable climate. I thought the *Strand Hotel*, on the way to the beach, had a friendly, warm atmosphere.

Although I am usually unmoved when I return to British resorts where I spent boyhood holidays, my first visit to Portrush evoked happy memories during the brief time I was there, a curious fact now that, in middle-age, I only like very small, unspoiled resorts. Not that Portrush is too large or spoiled—it is actually one of the best of the developed places in Ireland and England, with two excellent beaches, hotels of all categories in Lansdowne Crescent and other good positions, and all the normal resort amenities. The Royal Portrush Golf Club is internationally-known and visitors are welcome on three courses, for which green fees are nominal. There are fourteen tennis courts. Beyond the East Strand, the limestone White Rocks contain many caves.

Following the coast road, you next come to the little resort of Portballintrae, which has a good beach, three hotels and several boarding and guest houses. It is only a couple of miles from the well-known Giant's Causeway. While it is not unreasonable that this should be claimed as one of the world's wonders, some people do not go along with the charming legend of Finn MacCoul, the Irish giant who built the Causeway as a series of stepping stones on which to reach one of his enemies in Scotland. Incidentally, he is also credited with picking up a sizable land-mass and hurling it into the Irish Sea, thus creating both the Isle of Man and Lough Neagh.

A less fantastic explanation of the way in which almost half a mile of cliffs became split into tall, many-sided, regularly-shaped columns is given by Mr. H. Crookshank, in *True Story of the Giant's Causeway*, a booklet you will find on sale when you go there. The unique formation has its origins long after the time when, sixty million years ago, in the best geological tradition, Northern Ireland rose up out of the sea. Antrim aged a great deal before great cracks opened up and "great volumes of molten rock poured out of these, flooding all Antrim, much of Derry and probably a vast area to the north now beneath the sea. The molten rock was exposed to the weather, and in a relatively short time froze hard to form the black rock of basalt so familiar in the cliffs around the coast of Antrim." The booklet, a fascinating account of nature's engineering, is well worth reading.

At the point where you descend the road to the Causeway, there is a car park close to the hotel. As you come along the coast road to the Causeway, watch for a sign you could

219

easily miss, marking the short side road leading to the ruins of Dunluce Castle, perched dramatically on the cliff-edge. Its caretaker lives in the house opposite the little entrance gate. The castle is thought to date from 1300.

It has been abandoned since a room fell away into the sea about 1641. Among the many tales told of the castle is one which follows the usual romantic plot-line. This concerns the period, from 1580, when it belonged to the McQuillans. Maive Roe, the beautiful daughter of McQuillan Dhu, refused to marry the man he chose, was locked in the tower, later released when he relented, only to perish with her lover in stormy waters near the castle. The full story is given in the Portrush official guide, and ends with an unattributed poem I rather liked:

Now on its ruins slender sea-pink bloom,
And there, when night hangs down her veil of gloom,
The lonely bird of ocean finds its rest,
Hushed by the stormy billows of the west
That moan beneath its dark basaltic walls,
While rushing whirlwinds sweep its roofless halls.

From a point just west of Portrush you are on the Antrim Coast Road and now, moving on from the Causeway, you soon reach White Park Bay, probably the finest strand on the Ulster coastline, and consequently preserved unspoiled under the care of the National Trust. The white sand beach is a mile long with dunes and grass slopes behind. Here, and at the caves in the bay, many traces have been found of early inhabitants from the Neolithic Period to the Iron Age. A lane leads down to the shore, from which you can see the headlands of the Causeway, the little Sheep Island and the bigger bulk of Rathlin Island.

Next comes one of my two favourite coastal spots in Northern Ireland. This is Ballintoy, and the other, nearby, is Ballycastle. Driving along making for the latter, through one of those areas where the landscape lives up to its picturebook reputation, I saw a small cluster of buildings dominated by a tiny white church. Even after years of travel, apart from places which overwhelm me with their exciting characteristics, there are others which draw me magnetically with their simple beauty and peacefulness. These I am most loth to leave. They need not have anything great about them, nor the extra curiosity as in this case of a tower ornamented rather in the style of houses I have seen in Kano, Nigeria. On enquiry, I learned that this had no significance, was purely accidental. Ballintoy is a beauty spot. Go past the church, which dates from 1630, and down the short, winding road to the little cove where, alongside two or three rowing-boats, and a neat row of tiny, converted fishermen's cottages, you can spend a timeless afternoon or morning.

Bear this place in mind as an added attraction for the holiday I hope you will have at Ballycastle, six miles away. For me, this is the most pleasant resort in Northern Ireland —in fact, it is one of the places at which, as I have said to readers of other books in this series, we may meet, for I plan to go back there soon. One reason for my certain return is that the *Marine Hotel* is run by a rare fellow called Bernard Sherlock—rare because he combines efficiency in running his hotel with not merely the warm Irish welcome, but a gentle nature which seems to personalise even further the interest he takes in his guests. He is less rare only that in common with other hoteliers I have mentioned in these pages, he loves and sells you with enthusiasm the town, the district, the country. I was not surprised to discover that he is chairman of the urban council.

The *Marine* is a friendly hotel, situated on the shore road, at one end of an excellent beach. Its popularity is due to many things in addition to Mr. Sherlock—the comfortable lounges, the bar, the good food served in the recently converted restaurant where residents are separated from casual visitors, and the fact that Ballycastle, in a position protected from the east winds, is known as a dry and bracing corner of Ireland, suitable for winter as well as summer holidays.

Although important as a market town, Ballycastle is better-known as a seaside resort. The town is half-a-mile from the front, and the fact that they are apart from each other has given the resort its unspoiled character. In fact, you need not go into town, as, along the front from the *Marine*, there are several, well-stocked shops, one with a sub-post office. Beyond is the small harbour, from which there are 45-minute boat trips at 75 c. a head, to Rathlin Island, six miles across the water. On the island is Bruce's Cave, refuge of the famous king of Scotland, and the ruins of Bruce's Castle, claimed to be the place in which he learned from the spider's example. Ballycastle has a golf course of championship status, tennis courts, boating and sea angling facilities.

Near the golf course is the ruined Bun-na-Margy Abbey, burial place of the MacDonnells, Earls of Antrim. Dating from the fourteenth century, it is thought to be the last of its kind to be built before the Reformation. Beyond the sweep of the beach, along which is a cottage where Marconi lived, you can see Fair Head, six miles eastward. It is the highest promontory in the area, and extends for some three miles between Carrickmore Port and Murlough Bay. Glacial erratics can be seen in its vicinity, the most interesting being at "Grey Man's Path", so-called by the legend that the "Grey Man of the North Sea" walks up the ravine when, on stormy nights, he comes over from Scandinavia to Ireland. Fact instead of fiction is that the golden eagles

222

which once nested on Fair Head have returned—a small family has bred there recently.

You can go trout fishing in three lakes on Fair Head, with a permit issued by the Fisheries Office in Ballycastle. There are salmon fisheries on Torr Head. At a favourite picnic point overlooking Murlough Bay is a memorial to Roger Casement. Speed trials of liners built at the Harland and Wolff shipyards take place in the bay. A most interesting phenomenon six miles from Ballycastle on the way to Cushendun is Lough-A-Reema, the Vanishing Lake. This is a small lake which, with no regular frequency, disappears for a time, emerging as a spring a mile to the north-west, leaving a residual pool in the centre of a little plateau formed by the lake-alluvium, and revealing horizontal stratification. While there is no question of "now you see it, now you don't", you may be staying in the district long enough to see the change.

Near Ballintoy is Carrickarede, the "Rock in the Road" (of the salmon)—an island connected to the mainland by a "flying bridge" of rope cables supporting a pathway and lashed to rings in the rocks at each side of the chasm. The bridge is put up and opened on St. Patrick's Day, and taken down at the end of September. To the east, on Kenbane Head are the ruins of a castle; and those of Dunaney Castle stand on the cliffs less than a mile west of Ballycastle, six miles south of which lies Armoy, where a round tower, 35 feet high, is another of the local points of interest. In August, Ballycastle is the scene of the "Oul Lammas Fair", about which a song was written by John Macauley. This is a country-style fair, at which livestock and ponies, crown-and-anchor boards appear, and among the things on sale are dulse, a red edible seaweed, and "yellow man", a sticky toffee.

Visitors from Wales and certain parts of Hertfordshire

will be interested to note that Clough Williams Ellis, the distinguished Welsh architect, who designed Welwyn Garden City, contributed a great deal to the beauty of old Cushendun, set by one of the best bays on the Antrim section of the coast. It is a pity he was unable to prevent the management of the two comfortable waterside hotels, the *Bay* and the *Glendun*, from painting its company name in large letters on the sea wall. This apart, fortunately, the whole village was acquired a few years ago by the National Trust—I often reflect on the possible result of giving this admirable organisation full powers over all ministries, to the point where in fact it would be the permanent, non-party government. We could expect demolition of all the eye-searing structures that have been put up in a great many areas, a ban on new erections of the kind, a peaceful life of retreat for increasing numbers of the population who want it that way. Perhaps, with a unilateral effort paving the way, the Trust might achieve multilateral disarmament for the world!

I rather liked Cushendall, which comes next on the route southward. It has an excellent beach, lots of small trout in the Cushendall river which flows through its centre, and a golf course. Two good hotels, the *Cushendall* and the *Glens of Antrim*, are supplemented by a guest house and three boarding houses. This is a well-situated base from which to see the places of interest along the coastline on either side of the resort, especially Glenariff, the most beautiful of the Glens, close by on the south. I find it difficult to describe Glenariff adequately. According to the dictionary, a glen is a narrow valley, but this one presents a gentle, wide sweep towards the hills on either side, with a wonderful view of the sea beyond. Here, I can imagine, the legendary giant, Finn MacCoul, after chucking the Isle of Man into position, lay down to recuperate, and hollowed out this very lovely

27. Stormont, Belfast; seat of the Northern Ireland Parliament

28. The Mountains of Mourne, Co. Down

29. Pony trekking at Rostrevor, Co. Down

30. Derrymore House, Co. Armagh

valley. If you cannot see the other glens, although you should, don't miss this one.

Between the Glens and Belfast, either approaching the capital by remaining on the coast road, or cutting down through Ballyclare, I cannot pick out any place that is particularly attractive from the tourist's point of view. Whitehead is a not outstanding but reasonable small resort. Carrickfergus is notable only for its splendid Norman Castle, and the equally old hotel in the town, which contains in one of its walls, five feet thick, an underground passage of escape from the castle. Larne, at the end of the shortest sea route from Britain, has a resort area, with beaches, a good golf course, and other amenities. Even if you do not stay in Belfast, you must now pass through the capital before going south, whether you continue your journey near or on the coast, or divert further inland.

3. BELFAST

I am no longer the city-lover I was in my youth. Few cities now excite me as much as small places, and most of those that do are in Italy. While it may be unfair to draw comparisons with that country—although not entirely, as you can see from my Introduction—I am bound to say that, in common with many English cities, Belfast has few attractions for the tourist.

It has a University, and is the home of Harland and Wolff's, the world's biggest shipyard which, together with a complex of factories of various kinds, make it a great industrial and commercial centre. Because of this, most of what pleases the basic senses is on the edge and in the surrounds of the city. At its heart, however, is a splendid though modern (1906) City Hall, seen at its best in dusk light when soft floods are played on the dome and towers; St. Patrick's Church, in which can be seen, on special occasions, the Shrine of St. Patrick's Hand, a metal reliquary of the fifteenth century; St. Anne's Cathedral; the Botanic Gardens Park, which also contain the Ulster Museum, full of interesting exhibits; and in Witham Street, the Transport Museum.

This last houses Irish broad and narrow gauge railway and tramway stock (horse-drawn, electric, steam and diesel traction), motor coaches, veteran and vintage cars and motor-cycles. It also includes fire-engines, and a representative selection of private horse-drawn road vehicles.

On Cave Hill, four miles out, is a large natural park, with Belfast Castle standing on its eastern slopes. The castle grounds are open to visitors, and meals and refreshments can be obtained. In the nearby Bellevue Gardens are the Zoological Gardens and a miniature golf course. Not far away is Glengormley, where the Chimney Corner restaurant is worth noting. Also on Cave Hill is the place where Wolfe Tone and the northern leaders of the United Irishmen met in 1795, pledging themselves to the struggle for Ireland's independence. The most impressive sight, five miles from the centre, is Stormont, the Parliament Building, opened by the Duke of Windsor, when he was Prince of Wales, in 1932. It cost $3,000,000 and was provided by the British Government. The main approach is along a wide, processional avenue, and the Senate and House of Commons are among the apartments open to visitors. Also in the grounds are Stormont Castle, official residence of the Prime Minister; and the home of the Speaker of the House.

If you are a visiting industrialist, or for other reasons fortune has left you in a position to indulge a love of gracious living, take yourself off to either of two wonderful places I found near Belfast. Even if you are watching what's in the kitty, at least try them for a meal. Actually, although

226

dinner is *à la carte* in both places, each is reasonable for lunch. I rather suspect the stocks of its brochure have outlived the transformation which has taken place at the *Old Inn*, Crawfordsburn. Hotel brochures are often inaccurate. They tend to either exaggerate or fail to do justice to the places—in this case, the latter.

Ten miles from the capital, the *Old Inn* was once used by smugglers up to the end of the eighteenth century. Some secret hiding-places were discovered there, and the existence of others is suspected. Among pieces of fascinating old furniture is the big County Down dresser in the hall. In the unusual lounge is a brass chandelier originally presented to the parish church of Donaghadee in the seventeenth century, and an excellent specimen of the period. Two other interesting items are a pair of grindstones used by thirteenth-century monks and a wrought iron griddle and harnen stand, more than 200 years old, in the hall. This last was used in the primitive method of Irish baking to roast bannocks of bread. The thatched part of the building is the oldest, dating from about the end of the reign of Queen Elizabeth I and records of which show that it stood in its existing form in 1614. Owner Mrs. Eve White has tastefully decorated and furnished the lovely suites in the new wing, as a result of which they somehow manage to be both compact and spacious. There is also an old-world tea garden.

At Craigavad, one and a half miles from Holywood, on the south side of Belfast Lough, is the *Culloden Hotel*. Built by a Scotsman in 1876, it is a mansion in Scottish baronial style, standing in twelve acres of gardens and woodland, and was the official residence of the Bishop of Down for some years. Considerable use was made of handcut blocks of grey stone and sandstone in the original construction, and there is a tower rising to more than a

H*

hundred feet, from which an extensive view of the Down and Antrim coasts can be seen. The drawing room contains an eighteenth-century Adam fireplace, a Louis XV chandelier and the original delicate ceiling. In fact, the hotel is elegant throughout. It also has a ballroom, a garden bar and patio. The hard-working owners are Mr. and Mrs. Rutledge White—they constantly receive letters from overseas visitors who have appreciated their stay. Opposite the hotel, the Ulster Folk Museum was scheduled to open in July, 1964.

4. LOUGH NEAGH

Although I like lakes, the big ones are usually impersonal, and Lough Neagh, largest in Ireland or Britain, is in this category. The lake itself offers little to the tourist, but some of its tributaries are good salmon and trout fishing waters, and a mile from the Armagh shore is the ineptly named National Trust property, Coney Island, historically interesting as a retreat of St. Patrick, where an ancient round tower still stands, and all kinds of water-birds can be seen. Boats may be hired from Mr. George Forker, Milltown, Birches. Near Moneymore, on the Derry side of the lake, is a very attractive National Trust property, Springhill.

On the north-east is the town of Antrim, which has one of the two perfect round towers in Ireland, with a door nearly ten feet from the ground; and, at Pogue's Entry, the tiny cottage where Rev. Alexander Irvine, author of *My Lady of Chimney Corner* lived. Five miles away, north of the lake, is Randalstown, where a low road bridge and a railway bridge on a higher level cross the river in close parallel and with unusual effect. Here, too, is an old bleached linen mill, the only one in Ireland where the material is hand-painted.

5. THE REST OF THE NORTH

Bangor

Having already praised Portrush, I expect its citizens will allow me to say that Bangor is probably the foremost of the developed resorts; and those of Bangor should not mind me pointing out that, at least during the peak season period, their beach is crowded, mainly as a result of proximity to the capital. There are, in fact, several small beaches, but the most important is Ballyholme, in the bay of that name, at the eastern end. This stretches for a mile, and the four miles of seafront take it in together with Bangor Bay and Smelt Mill Bay.

The sea-water Pickie Pool, one of the best enclosed swimming pools in the country, is an outstanding amenity, equipped as it is with diving and spring boards, as well as seating for more than 1,000 spectators. I was told that even when the beach is crowded, the town's lovely parks are peaceful places to visit, and running inland from Smelt Mill Bay, the harbour at Strickland's Glen is another quiet and attractive spot.

Several golf courses, putting and bowling greens and numerous tennis courts are among the amenities. There are also facilities for sea-angling, rowing boats can be hired, and motor-boat trips can be made to Carrickfergus, the Copeland Islands and Belfast Lough. Historically, it is interesting to note that Bangor had its origins in the monastery founded there by St. Comgall in the year 555.

Down and around

Going down the Down coast and then around the rest of the places of interest in the county, begin with the six-mile drive from Bangor through lovely, contrasted scenery, to Donaghadee, where there is good bathing and fishing in and near the harbour, an open-air swimming pool, a golf course, tennis courts, bowling greens, and a large park within which you will find these facilities. Boats and boat trips are available here, too—incidentally, the compass trials take place in the bay. Donaghadee has four hotels, one guest house and two boarding houses.

On the beach at Ballywalter, twelve miles southward, is the airy new studio of the Irish School of Landscape Painting, where Holiday Art Courses are held—I have described these fully in Part One. At the mouth of Strangford Lough is the little fishing port and resort of Portaferry, also a yachting centre. A ferry takes passengers to the small town of Strangford on the other side of the Lough entrance. Three National Trust properties near the Lough and open to the public are Castlewood, Mount Stewart Gardens and Rowallane.

At Saul, where St. Patrick landed in A.D. 432 to begin his mission in Ireland, there are only slight remains of the church he founded, but on the slopes above the village is a small modern memorial church of Mourne granite with a round tower belfry. A mile to the west is an enormous granite statue of the saint, at the top of a hill, and on a terrace lower down, Mass is celebrated each year. I liked the busy town of Downpatrick, two miles from Saul. In the grounds of its lovely cathedral is the grave of the saint. Three miles from the town are the beautifully-located ruins of Inch Abbey.

Where the Mountains of Mourne actually sweep down to the sea, specifically at the foot of Slieve Donard, is the resort of Newcastle, where a boating lake, a swimming pool, tennis courts, bowling greens and one of Ireland's best golf courses are to be found. Also here, at the water's edge, is the *Slieve Donard Hotel*, one of those transport authority hotels which, big and old-fashioned though they are in many respects, have made enough concessions to modernity to retain a following. The Slieve Donard Mountain, Tollymore Forest Park and Dundrum Castle all provide interesting, enjoyable excursions.

Also in the shadow of the Mournes is the little fishing village at which I could not resist humming a couplet, "Annalong, Down-along." In fact, Annalong, County Down, has a tiny, peaceful harbour, a lot of good scenery around, and a guest house. Apart from being an anchorage for fishing-boats, it is a place in which Mourne granite is dressed for export.

Between Annalong and Kilkeel, you will see Silent Valley signposted. This is the Belfast main reservoir, in an impressive setting. Entry can be made only with a permit from Belfast City and District Water Commissioners. Fishing and granite dressing, as in Annalong, are the main occupations of Kilkeel, a well-kept little town which I liked very much, especially for its harbour, where I took some pictures of its exciting-looking fleet. It has a sandy beach, too, and offers excellent sea angling on the shore and from the pier. There are brown trout in the Kilkeel and Whitewater rivers, as well as sea trout and salmon in season. I stayed at the *Kilmorey Arms*, a small hotel with gaily-converted very comfortable rooms where, although I had a disappointing meal, I believe the food is normally quite good. The town has an annual Prawn Festival in June. West of Kilkeel, the road runs along the shore of Carlingford Lough, on which Rostrevor and Warrenpoint are two resorts. Rostrevor, especially the *Roxboro Hotel*, is a pony-trekking centre. Newry, a few miles inland from Warrenpoint, is an industrial town where the town hall is built over the river.

There are several places in good settings, with various amenities, but which have limited hotel accommodation. One of these is Ballynahinch (not to be confused with the

231

Galway spot of the same name) which is historically important as the scene of the last stand of the United Irishmen in the north in 1798, and of the death of Betsy Grey and two men who fought for the insurgents. They were killed while retreating, by a group of yeomanry.

Armagh

Parts of every country must escape both the writer's and the reader's attention, some because it is unnecessary to see them, also because it is a physical impossibility to cover every corner. What a travel writer aims to do is point up the "musts" and lead the way to areas and centres which are worth exploring. I have tried to do just that here, and I must mention one more place you should visit to complete your tour.

The cathedral city of Armagh, ecclesiastical capital of Ireland, dates from A.D. 443, when St. Patrick established his first church on the hill of Ard Macha, from which the town is named. Historically, it goes back further, to 300 B.C. when the warrior Queen Macha founded a fort there. It is a pleasant town with well-laid out streets, some fine Georgian and Regency houses, and a park set between two rows of houses. The library dates from 1781, and there is an old, international observatory.

A mile and a half from Newry, on the Armagh side, is one of the most attractive buildings in the country. Derry-more House is almost the only survivor of the small thatched-roof mansion houses once favoured by the minor Irish gentry, and restored to its eighteenth-century character. In what is called the Treaty Room is an unusual shamrock-shaped table, supported by a harp, upon which, in this room, the Act of Union is said to have been drafted, and upon which King George V actually signed the Declaration granting the Constitution of Northern Ireland in 1921.

232

TAILPIECE

I have included a great deal of information for anglers. I make no apology. Ireland offers peace to everyone, but is particularly an angler's paradise. In fact, I got the bug there myself. Although I don't really need any added incentive to keep returning, the combination of lake, line and rod, and all that wonderful quiet, are likely to win me over very frequently. So I warn everyone now. If there comes a time when I am wanted and cannot be found, you'll know I got off the hook. "Gone fishing". In Ireland. On a one-way ticket. I'll be the one that got away.

PART FIVE

APPENDICES

APPENDICES

Irish Tourist Offices

NEW YORK   Ireland House, 33 East 50th St.
                              (Tel.: PLaza 3/30158/0161)

CHICAGO   135 South La Salle Street
                              (Tel.: ANdover 3/3773)

MONTREAL   2100 Drummond Street
                              (Tel.: VIctor 9–5289)

SAN FRANCISCO   Room 899, 681 Market Street
                              (Tel.: SUtter 1–5688/9)

In Dublin, information can be obtained from the Bureau of the Irish Tourist Association, 15 Upper O'Connell Street, between the hours of 9 a.m. and 7.30 p.m. on Mondays to Fridays, 9 a.m. and 5 p.m. on Saturdays, from May to September. The Room Reservation Service is open until 10 p.m. every night except Sunday, and during winter, the I.T.A. office is open during normal office hours. The Tourist Information Centre in Creation Arcade, Grafton Street, is open from 9.30 a.m. to 5.30 p.m. on Mondays to Fridays, from May to September. The Brown Thomas store, also in Grafton Street, has an Information Bureau, open from 9 a.m. to 5.30 p.m. except on Saturdays, when it closes at 1 p.m.

Airline Offices

Irish International Airlines Offices in North America and Australia:

BOSTON   66/68 Arlington Street
                              (Tel.: HUbbard 2–2025)

CHICAGO   Room 608, Champlain Bldg., 37 South Wabash Avenue   (Tel.: FRanklin 2–2214)

CLEVELAND	Room 958, Hanna Bldg., 1422 Euclid Avenue (Tel.: CHerry 1–7516/8)
DALLAS	Suite 1703 Vaughn Bldg., 1712 Commerce Street (Tel.: RIverside 2–6128)
DETROIT	Suite 1508, Washington Boulevard Bldg. (Tel.: 962–7755)
LOS ANGELES	510 West Sixth Street (Tel.: 624–6061)
MONTREAL	Place Ville Marie (Tel.: 875–5350)
NEW YORK	572 Fifth Avenue (Tel.: PLaza 7–9200)
PHILADELPHIA	Room 908, 1518 Walnut Street (Tel.: KIngsley 6–4224)
SAN FRANCISCO	681 Market Street (Tel.: EXbrook 7–5863)
SYDNEY	Suite 4, Park House, 187–191 Macquarie Street (Tel.: 285392)
TORONTO	Imperial Life Tower, 25 Adelaide Street, East (Tel.: 362–6565)
WASHINGTON	1028 Connecticut Ave., N.W. (Tel.: 296–4550)

British European Airways Office is at 40 Upper O'Connell Street, Dublin. Tel.: British Bookings, 71831; European, 42591; Flight Information, 46851.

Embassies in Dublin

BRITISH	39 Merrion Square (Tel.: 65196)
CANADIAN	92 Merrion Square (Tel.: 63261)
AMERICAN	15 Merrion Square (Tel.: 65682)

* * *

Northern Ireland Tourist Information Bureaux

The Northern Ireland Tourist Board has a Tourist Information Centre at 6 Royal Avenue, Belfast 1. Tel.: 31222/6. The offices of the Board are at 10 Royal Avenue, and its London Enquiry

Bureau is c/o Office of the Ulster Agent, 13 Regent Street, London, S.W.1. Tel.: WHItehall 0651–5. Enquiries can also be made in London at the offices of the British Travel and Holidays Association, 64/65 St. James's Street, S.W.1. Tel.: MAYfair 9191.

In the United States of America, enquiries can be made at the offices of the British Travel Association:

680 Fifth Avenue, New York, 19, N.Y.

(Tel.: CIrcle 5–2800)

612 South Flower Street, Los Angeles, 17, California.

(Tel.: MAdison 3–8196)

39 South La Salle Street, Chicago 3, Illinois.

(Tel.: DEarborn 2–6744)

INDEX

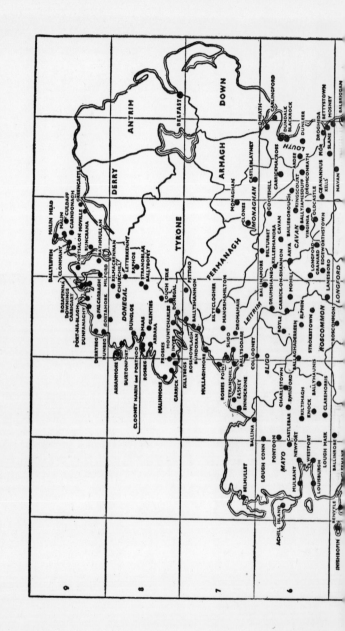